D1202504

MOURNING
JOURNEY

MOURNING JOURNEY

Spiritual Guidance for Facing Grief, Death & Loss

Dennis Young

DPI

DISCIPLESHIP
PUBLICATIONS
INTERNATIONAL

Mourning Journey
©2003 by Discipleship Publications International
2 Sterling Road, Billerica, Mass. 01863

All rights reserved.
No part of this book may be duplicated, copied,
translated, reproduced or stored mechanically or
electronically without specific, written permission of
Discipleship Publications International.

All Scripture quotations, unless indicated, are taken from
the NEW INTERNATIONAL VERSION.
Copyright ©1973, 1978, 1984 by the International Bible
Society. Used by permission of Zondervan Publishing House.
All rights reserved.

The "NIV" and "New International Version" trademarks
are registered in the United States Patent Trademark
Office by the International Bible Society.
Use of either trademark requires the permission of
the International Bible Society.

Printed in the United States of America

Cover and Interior Design: Jennifer Matienzo

ISBN: 1-57782-189-0

Contents

Acknowledgments

I would like to acknowledge a number of people without whose support, encouragement and assistance this book would not have been written.

I would like to thank Randy McKean for his love for the church and his leadership and foresight to meet emerging needs. Because of hearts like his, the church will always receive the kind of attention that God wants for it.

I would like to thank Gordon Ferguson who has encouraged me to serve the church in this area of need and to write this book.

I would like to thank my wife, Elaine, and my kids, Annie, Dean and John. Elaine has done it all, from editing to coaching to making sure this happened. I love you and thank you! Thank you to my children for giving me the okay to write and for living with a dad who is known around the neighborhood as the "guy who talks about death and dying."

I would like to thank my parents for doing the hard work of raising me and introducing me to God. Thank you for always loving and caring for my family and me over the years.

I would like to thank Kelly Petre and the DPI staff for their desire to publish this book from the first mention of it. I hope their constant encouragement and expectation will not go unrewarded.

I would like to thank God, before whom we will all appear some day: thank you for salvation in a dying world and for a life that will not end in death.

Introduction
Mourning Journey

Fourteen years later, I can still see the day as clearly as the computer screen in front of me. My wife and I were grabbing a quick dinner before church at the only Mexican food restaurant in Northampton, Massachusetts, when a good friend of mine came through the door (how he knew I was there I do not know) and asked if he could speak to me outside. It was one of those requests that you have a funny feeling about right from the start. When we were outside the restaurant he said, "Dennis, your dad has had a heart attack, and they are not sure how he is doing. Your mom is waiting for you to call her back at my place."

As my wife joined us and we crossed the street to my friend's apartment, the situation back home was growing more serious than we knew.

I had anticipated receiving this kind of call for a while. My dad's mother and father had both died of heart attacks, and my dad was in a high stress job that kept him running from plane to plane and place to place. I quickly went into the "let's get a plan" mode, directing my mother and sister over the phone to get into the car and drive the seven hours to the hospital where dad was being treated. (He had flown into the airport in San Antonio, Texas, on business and upon seeing his ashen face in the rearview mirror, had instructed the cab driver to find the nearest hospital.) I told them that I would locate my brother (we were both living in Massachusetts) and we would be on the next flight out.

It took all night to locate my brother, but by the next morning my wife, he and I were on the way to Texas. I must say that this was one of the longest plane flights I have ever taken. I think I prayed the whole way. I begged, bargained, promised and pleaded. I sat confused, dazed, depressed, angered and anxious. Everything went through my mind—from memories of home life to hearing the bad news that he didn't make it. At times I felt panic and that I too was having a heart attack. Death was not a topic I had discussed extensively with anyone. I had no reference for it, no teaching on it, no way to know how to deal with it, and now was not the time I wanted to begin.

I remember eventually stepping out of the airport into the hot Texas sun, but everything else is still a blur in my memory until we reached the room where my mom and sister were waiting. I was so grateful to hear that my dad was still alive. He had survived the attack, but now the question was how he would do going forward. I remember great relief, but also an accompanying amount of stress. I was thankful to God and at the same time mad at my dad for getting himself and us into such a situation to begin with. I had experienced deaths before, but this event brought death a lot closer to home than I was ready for.

Over the ensuing years, I experienced a continual series of similar events with both friends and family—from accidents to medical emergencies, from terminal illnesses to unexpected deaths. In various ways they have all contributed to my own understanding and growth as well as to the writing of this book. In the process of all of this I have found in people both the extremes of a complete lack of understanding about grief and loss to ritual responses that tend to be unrelatable and seemingly out of touch. Knowing that our Western society does not deal well with death in general, I believe there is a need for a spiritual awareness and understanding of death, dying and mourning. Hopefully this book will meet some of this need and in the long run help people to stay faithful to God through times of great suffering, loss and grief.

This book is addressed to several different types of people. First, to those who are grieving the loss of someone in death. Second, to those who are helping and supporting those who are in grief. Third, to those who are dying. Fourth, to those who are supporting them. And last, to all of us who have gone through or will go through loss and grief in any or all of the above-mentioned ways. In short, this book is addressed to all of us.

To those of you who are weary and burdened from the suffering that death and dying bring, I hope that what I have written will in some way validate the pain you feel and the struggles you face. I hope it encourages you to fight harder, to have the faith to overcome, and to never give up on God. With this in mind, I open this book with the encouraging words of the apostle Paul:

> Indeed, in our hearts we felt the sentence of death. But this happened that we might not rely on ourselves but on God, who raises the dead. He has delivered us from such a deadly peril, and he will deliver us. On him we have set our hope. (2 Corinthians 1:9–10)

Interspersed throughout the book will be life-experience sections called "My Story," written by those who have experienced the loss of someone in their lives and are living through the grief and mourning process. They will tell their stories and they will in so doing respond to two questions:

1. What was most difficult for me in experiencing my loss?

2. What helped the most as people gave me support during my loss?

My hope is that shared pain will bring shared healing. It is comforting to know that we are not alone in our grief and to know that death and dying experiences are common to all of mankind.

In reading this book, please keep these things in mind: First, it is not an exhaustive study on death and dying. It does, however, cover a wide range of topics, many of which are touched on but not discussed in great detail. To compensate for this, I have tried to direct you to books and writings from credible professionals who work in the field of death, dying and mourning. These resources can provide you with more information for your particular concerns and needs. I have included references within each chapter, as well as a resource list and bibliography in the back of the book. I must caution you, however, that some of these authors might hold different spiritual convictions than you do, and they will not always agree with each other about every aspect of grief, death and loss. Therefore, use wisdom when reading these books, and realize that the issues involved can be complex and the various approaches more or less helpful for your particular situation.

Second, if you have picked up this book in order to help someone who has experienced death or loss, I would encourage you to resist the temptation to jump to the "helping" chapter without reading the earlier, foundational chapters on loss, grief and mourning. The opening chapters are vitally important for understanding the mind-set of those you wish to help.

Third, this book is somewhat a translation. I have attempted to look at the world of death and dying not only in its clinical, academic and working environment—but from a spiritual perspective. I have included thoughts from this perspective for you to consider at the end of many of the chapters. The purpose of these thoughts is to aid in thinking through the information, facts and opinions from a spiritual point of view. Hopefully these suggestions will help us to think and respond more like Jesus as we face the challenges brought on by death. Certainly, none of us looks forward to the loss of friends or family, but with God's promise of life we have hope that can cause us to rise above the pain and heartache of loss and continue to live meaningful lives.

Fourth, don't run away from reading this book. All of us need to understand, at least in a general way, what is presented here. You will not find death to be a topic that is often discussed in classrooms or coffee shops, on fairways or in very many homes—but it ought to be. As Christians we must be comfortable with, if not looking forward to, the future that death begins for us. We need to be reminded that we live in "jars of clay" (2 Corinthians 4:7), and we must be able to discuss death with a degree of understanding and confidence. Then we will be able to sing honestly, "This world is not my home; I'm just a-passing through."

I am forever thankful that God desires to be our companion as we each take our mourning journeys in life.

Editor's Note: Throughout the book you will find that the pronouns "he" and "him" are used in some places and "she" and "her" are used in others. This is done to avoid the clumsiness of the "he or she" and "him and her" construction.

1
Loss

John is a young friend of mine. He is a tall, thin, active teenager who has an infectious smile and loves to take me on in sports. Recently, he lost his father to cancer. His dad's death, though certainly John's greatest loss, is one of many losses in this young man's life.

To begin with, John suffered loss at an early age when he was placed in an orphanage. Most of us can imagine the pain of a child without a family. Fortunately, he was adopted by an American family and brought to the United States, an encouraging development to be sure, but one that resulted in the loss of his native country and culture and the prospect of ever knowing who his real family was. However, his adoptive father, the one who recently died, was a compassionate man who made John his own son and loved him unconditionally.

John's childhood years were like those of many other children, filled with school, friends and family fun. But with the advent of his early teen years, things changed. John's dad was diagnosed with cancer. The father who had created a new world for John now found his own world coming apart. The spiritual answers that were provided did not always make sense to a young teenager who was understanding that his father was very sick and could possibly die. At that point he did not know what was to follow: a series of losses which, for the most part, would take his father from him long before he actually died.

The relationship between a father and a teenage son can be challenging in the best of circumstances, but having cancer adds a whole new dimension. Teens, although striving for independence, still depend on the experience, love and guidance of their parents. Increasingly, John felt that he had to compete in order to get these needs met—not with siblings or his dad's work, but with the cancer itself. Its regimens, therapies, hospital visits and mental demands vied for his dad's time and attention, and their father-son relationship took a back seat. John wanted to play basketball with his dad. He wanted his help with homework or just to hang out and watch a movie together. But battling cancer became such an intense struggle for his dad that they began to slip apart. And when they were together, they failed to talk about the difficult situation and how it was affecting them. John was left to figure out what was going on from his mother and others, but not from any real discussion with his dad. Little by little he was being shut out of his dad's life and his dad's struggle with the disease. Cancer was becoming John's enemy as well as his dad's. It was not only killing his father; it was killing his relationship with his father as well. At times it was too much for him to bear.

In an effort to gain attention and to get the relationship back, John found himself acting out on occasion or burying himself in activities. His attitude at home became difficult. Both parents noticed his increased irritability and lack of cooperation. Playing sports allowed him to escape from the reality of the world he was living in and at the same time was a plea for someone to notice him. However, the attention he desperately sought by participating in events could not be given by a father who could rarely attend them. His dad's declining condition kept him from doing the father-and-son things that John so desperately wanted. Cancer was giving him very little room to be part of a relationship that John needed the most.

His dad died after his long and brave fight with cancer. Fortunately, before this happened, John and his dad were able to recover some of their relationship. They went on a few family trips together and had some real discussions about his dad's declining health and the future. This was very important to John. Finally, he felt that he was connecting with his dad. He had the chance to express things about their relationship and now heard firsthand about his dad's view of the disease and the battle he was waging against it. John now realized some peace in having a real and vital talk with the most important man in his life. By the end, they had done some important work in their relationship that not even the disease could take away.

After his father's death, John and the rest of the family experienced some relief from the difficulties that disease brings to any household; but of course, there was also the absence of the man who had led the family in sickness and in health. John felt the immediate loss of his dad's love, help, guidance, support and leadership. Equally as difficult, and harder to express in words, was facing the prospect of numerous future losses—losses that would come as a result of walking through life without a dad and all that relationship would have meant over time. To many, it appeared that John had only lost his dad; but in reality, his losses are far more than most people will ever know.

Loss Is the Beginning

Like John, we will all experience loss, and loss is the beginning of the grieving process. It is the beginning of mourning. It is also the beginning of much more, such as learning about God, ourselves and the people around us. In loss, we will all face suffering, surviving and the chance to live out our Christianity in the midst of some of the most challenging circumstances in life.

A dictionary defines loss as "the harm resulting from losing." Professor Charles Corr puts it simply when he writes,

> When anyone experiences the loss of someone or some thing that is valued, he or she is harmed. Something important is taken away, often abruptly and in a hurtful way.[1]

Think about losses you have suffered and see if this statement is true. If you have ever felt robbed or deprived, you have felt loss. Loss is deprivation. It is being deprived of someone or something we once had. Loss occurs in many ways and takes away from us in different ways. For example, when someone we love dies, we lose not just a person, but dreams, fun, friends, children, caring, loving, joy and the future that would have been. This is loss.

Furthermore, if we had a relationship with the deceased, we have become "bereaved." "Bereavement" is simply another way of saying that we have suffered a loss. The root word of this rather old-fashioned term is "to rob." When we lose someone dear to us, we have been robbed, deprived of that which we once had.

Loss Is Part of Life

The writer of Ecclesiastes wrote, "There is a time for everything...a time to be born and a time to die" (Ecclesiastes 3:1–2). Loss is a part of this life; it always has been and always will be. There is no escaping it. I state this obvious fact because many times when we experience a loss through death, we act as if something unknown or unfair has happened to us. Yet even God himself would remind us that we came into this world with an "internal clock" that will eventually stop, ending our lives here on earth. Therefore, we should expect loss; but by accepting this fact, we also have an opportunity to consider it, prepare for it and embrace it, rather than run from it or deny it.

Loss Is Painful

Loss resulting from death is painful because there is no possibility of recovery. Once lost, there is no way to get the person back. The death of a loved one is probably the most difficult thing we will experience in life. Losing relationships brings pain. The love, care and concern that we had been giving and receiving can no longer be experienced with that person. All that our relationship was or could have been is gone. The deeper our attachments are to a loved one, the deeper we will experience the loss. We need to expect the pain that comes from loss and the difficulty in dealing with it. As Joan Arnold says,

> Dealing with feelings of loss does not come easily. It is the hurt in life that we hope to soothe, hope to quiet and cover, hope to repair and recover from as quickly as possible.[2]

Relationship loss as a result of death could be imagined as having an arm or leg severed with no hope of reattachment. We would feel intense pain, not only from it being severed from our body, but also from the knowledge of having to live without it for the rest of our lives. This type of pain is the "harm" that loss brings.

Loss Changes Us

Losing relationships and experiencing the pain that goes along with the loss will change us. It will change our thinking about life and how we live. It will change our view of the world, and it may change our beliefs about God. Loss may bring about changes in our occupation, our home and our friendships. It will have an impact on us. Our lives will be different. However, as you go through this book and get in touch with the challenges and difficulties of loss and grief, you will hopefully become convinced that even through the pain, good can come. In the midst of deprivation and hurt, loss can present us with opportunities to grow. It can teach us something new about ourselves, about our lives and about adapting and overcoming in ways that we may never have thought possible. As one writer put it, "What matters is not what life does to you, but rather what you do with what life does to you."[3]

Types of Loss

When someone dies, it is important to know that there are additional losses other than the death itself. These losses will require mourning as well as compassion and help for those who experience them. Losses can be grouped into three different categories.

Physical Loss—The actual tangible loss of a person to death.

Symbolic Loss—An abstract loss such as the loss of a great "father figure" to the community.

Secondary Loss—Consequences of physical and symbolic losses, such as losing a father-son relationship when the father becomes debilitatingly ill or losing a day-to-day partner in child-raising when a husband or wife dies.

When a loved one dies, physical loss is often the most obvious loss to an outside observer. However, the associated symbolic and secondary losses are painful as well. These related losses must be acknowledged and also grieved. For instance, in our story at the beginning of the chapter, John's secondary losses included losing a significant and unique relationship in his life; losing a link to his past, including his childhood, memories and family history; losing his friend, coach, provider and more. When his dad died, John could have lost his home, his neighborhood friends and his school if his mother had not been able to pay the mortgage. And not least of all, he lost whatever future he might have had with his dad, such as celebrating holidays, getting married or seeing his father become a grandfather to his own children.

Spiritual Notes

Prepare Ourselves

For whatever reason, we can often think that loss only happens to other people. All people experience loss.

Christians will experience loss. Children, parents, friends, coworkers and others in our lives will die. They will die of cancer, heart disease, rare and unusual diseases, accidents and catastrophes. No one will be exempt. We will lose friends and family who are not Christians (discussed later in this chapter) as well as those who are. If it is other Christians that we lose, we will have hope for their future as well as a better foundation from which to spiritually and healthily work through our grief. We will see and feel the victory of a life lived out God's way. This is not to say the loss will be easy, but we have spiritual tools with which to deal with it. As Paul wrote, we will not grieve as others do because we are confident of the spiritual destiny of our Christian brothers and sisters (1 Thessalonians 4:13–18).

Considering the possibility of losing someone close to us can cause us to evaluate our relationship with God. If our faith at present for us is only an adherence to the rules, a church setting, friends and relationships, but not a deep connection with God himself (Matthew 22:37–40), then a confrontation with death will show our relationship with God for what it really is. If we are not currently experiencing what God would call a close relationship, then we should get help now: get into our Bibles and get on our knees and get connected with God before the day of trouble comes (Ecclesiastes 12:1–7).

Face the Challenges to Our Faith

Loss challenges our spiritual foundation. It naturally calls for a reordering or a reorganization of our worldview, since with the loss, our world has changed. As Christians, we find that loss can cause us to question our faith and belief in God. It does this by raising questions that are generally in the form of "Why?" such as "Why didn't God heal him?" or "Why did she have to die when she had young children?" or "Why did our child die?" We should expect these questions to spring up and even continue for a while.

Loss can challenge our faith by launching us into a struggle with God. This happens as the loss challenges our convictions, our commitment, our beliefs and our relationship with God. As we strive to find meaning in the loss, we may attempt to put God on trial for answers and explanations about the death and the deceased (see John 11:32 for an example). This challenge strikes at the heart of what we really believe about God and if we will continue to believe it as we work through the loss.

At the appropriate time we will need to face all these challenges. However, we must first make sure we are ready. We have to give ourselves time and be sure we are in a supportive environment with good spiritual relationships around us before moving ahead. We must be patient, recognizing that the initial period of grief is intense and great mental and emotional upheaval comes with it. We should expect some of the questions, but we can make a conscious decision that we will deal with them when we feel we are ready. As we continue to make decisions to trust God, he will gently guide us through our questions by not always giving us answers, but by always giving us himself.

How do we face these types of challenges?

Face Challenges with God

God will help us through loss, grief and mourning, and he will help us through terminal illness. In the midst of pain and spiritual upheaval God moves closer to help us live through our losses. The Psalmist says, "The Lord is close to the brokenhearted and saves those who are crushed in spirit" (Psalm 34:18). God's heart goes out to us in our loss. He himself has experienced great loss and knows how we feel in times of grief and mourning. He is not looking at us from some distant place, wondering how we are doing; rather, he draws close to walk with us through our difficult times. David says, "Even though I walk through the valley of the shadow of death,...you are with me" (Psalm 23:4). Paul says in Romans chapter eight that nothing can separate us from God or keep him from loving us, not even death. And the Hebrew writer reassures us when he quotes the Father saying, "Never will I leave you; never will I forsake you" (Hebrews 13:5). It is clear that even though we may waver, doubt and question, he continues to love us and help us. This is the compassion of God. He understands our experience and he is moved to help. "As a father has compassion on his children, so the Lord has compassion on those who fear him; for he knows how we are formed, he remembers that we are dust" (Psalm 103:13–14).

Not only does God respond to us with compassion, but he strengthens us for the fight. Paul says, "I have learned to be content whatever the circumstances.... I can do everything through him who gives me strength" (Philippians 4: 11, 13). God has done many things to strengthen us and ensure our success as Christians. To begin with, he has given us his indwelling Spirit, who "helps us in our weakness" (Romans 8:26). In other words, the Spirit gives us the power to deal with the challenges and difficulties that we face in this life, death obviously being one of the most difficult. Paul helps us to understand this power and its availability to Christians when he equates it with the power that raised Jesus from the dead

(Romans 8:11). Peter explains that the source of the power is God and that he gives it to us as we need it: "His divine power has given us everything we need for life and godliness" (2 Peter 1:3–4). It is God's strengthening from within by his Spirit that enables us to live through loss and mourning and to stay faithful to him through the most spiritually-challenging times of our lives.

God has given us his word to strengthen us. Through his word he reassures us in times of trouble and provides answers and meaning. Scriptures speak to us during all aspects of grief and mourning. They encourage, comfort, counsel, clarify, identify, normalize, support and bring hope to us during loss. God strengthens us through the stories, truths, teachings and examples in the Bible. From the pain and despair of Job to the emotional entreaties and psalms of David to the revelation of a new and eternal body by Paul, God speaks to our needs with reassuring words.

Eventually, truths will emerge from God's scriptures that can help us find meaning in our loss (see chapter 4 for additional thoughts). Sometimes the truth may be that there is no answer as to the "why" of our loss and that faith is required to move on. In other circumstances, we may find that teachings, truths or time reveal things that help us understand our loss better and provide a greater meaning, helping to reassure us about life and God. When all is said and done, we will want to come through these challenging times close to God, and that can happen when we face loss with his help.

Face Challenges with Spiritual Help

Our comfort will need to come from the Bible, from times spent alone with God and with other spiritual people. Our understanding will grow over time as we are able to listen to and take in God's word. The more we are able to study what God says and thinks about our situation, the better we will do spiritually in the long run (again, see chapter 4).

Also, we should get help from mature Christians who can assist us as we walk through the process of making important decisions or drawing conclusions. Staying close to spiritual friends and family can help keep us strong through loss. Find those you can trust and talk with and get open. Try not to let yourself get isolated during these times.

Face Challenges with Hope

Finally, in dealing with challenges to our faith, we must be open to the possibility for growth and transformation. The Bible is a continual story of God's intervention and salvation in men's darkest moments. Even in the most traumatic deaths, God can move to renew hope, conviction and life (see 2 Corinthians 1:8–10). After a loss, we may not feel that any growth is foreseeable, but as we work through the loss and stay anchored to God, we will find that transformation is possible. We can become deeper people spiritually. This is not to say that it will happen overnight, but as Paul says, "Though outwardly we are wasting away, yet inwardly we are being renewed day by day. For our light and momentary troubles are achieving for us an eternal glory that far outweighs them all" (2 Corinthians 4:16–17).

Especially Difficult Losses

Deaths of those who are not Christians. We are speaking here of deaths that happen outside our belief about what God and his word say about salvation. These types of deaths may present some particularly difficult challenges (1 Samuel 15:35). There can be more questions, more "What if's?" and subsequently, more grief.

In these situations, it is difficult to come to grips with someone's spiritual destiny at the time of their death, especially if we were somewhat aware of their relationship with God. We need to get help from others when working through spiritual issues like these (Matthew 18:19–20). Also, as I said earlier, we should wait until we are ready to deal with this question and then study the Bible for answers (and do so in a spiritually supportive environment). God's word must give us our perspective when working through this loss as well (2 Timothy 3:16–17). The challenge will be to hold on, through a difficult time, to what God has written, rather than change our thinking to accommodate the emotional crisis we are experiencing (Ephesians 4:14). The closer to God we are and the more grounded in his word we are, the better chance we have of working through the loss in a spiritual way (Psalm 119:111–112). We must decide not to allow ourselves to draw any conclusions regarding someone's spiritual destiny until we are mentally and emotionally ready to do so. And we must always remember that God is the final judge, not us or anyone else. Ultimately everyone must be placed in his hands.

The death of a child. We will address this heartrending experience more in chapter 10. The death of a child at any age is incredibly difficult, whether sudden, accidental or due to disease. The death of a child under the age of accountability (meaning the time a child is old enough to be accountable to God for his actions) will still be a hard death to deal with, even if you believe that God's word teaches that such a child is saved. Do not assume that because parents, friends and family members believe the child is with God, they will therefore view the death with a happy, courageous and victorious heart. A child has died. Yes, there is hope; but there is also tremendous grief.

Other types of "complicated" deaths. Some deaths have other factors present and can be especially difficult to deal with, such as deaths from AIDS, suicide, homicide or accident. More specific types of help may be required to work through the challenges that losses of this type present (see chapter 10).

Loss is a beginning point. It is what sets in motion events, emotions, changes and more. It is a natural part of life that, though painful, is transforming as well. Spiritually, we should be ready to face loss as best we can. Loss brings with it some challenging thoughts and questions, but also advances the opportunity to deepen our spirituality and draw us closer to God.

2
Grief

Her name is Eulah Mae Kilpatrick, but people call her Sue. She is my grandmother. She is ninety-five years old, and she was married to my grandfather for more than sixty-five years. They were married very young by today's standards. They faced many hardships through the years, including a Great Depression, two World Wars and the challenge of raising a family and farming cotton in the hard country of West Texas. Living on a farm in a small community, they worked together, ate together, went to church together and even fished together. They were each other's constant companion.

My grandparents' farm was my summer home away from home. They provided my brother and me enough memories to last us a lifetime. As they grew older and their health began to deteriorate, the rigors of farm life became too much for them. So, around the time I left home and moved to another part of the country, they left the farm and moved in with my family. One day I received the phone call telling me my grandfather was sick and in the hospital. And very soon after, he died.

My grandfather was just about to turn ninety when he died. The hospital staff commented on how physically strong he was right up to the end. For this reason, his death took us a bit by surprise. We thought, *After all, look at what he has lived through up till now.*

I flew down for the funeral. I thought it was hard for me, but I realized it was really hard for my mother and her small family—now consisting of just her and her brother and mother.

We drove out to the little community where they had lived. The service was attended by an ever-shrinking group of mostly gray-haired people who had come to say good-bye. During the service I was more attentive to my mom than my grandmother until the time came to close the casket. It was then that I witnessed an outburst of grief like none I had ever seen before. It was the most painful sound of talking and crying that I have ever heard—and it came from my grandmother, who could not let go. After having shared all those years together, she was now being asked to say good-bye to my grandfather at the end of a forty-five minute service. I wept as I watched her express her deepest emotions for someone with whom she had spent essentially her whole life.

Finally she was able to allow the casket to be closed, and we drove with her to the place where he was to be buried. After the burial, she stayed there for a while just to talk with him. It was tremendously sad to sit and watch the parting of a relationship that had endured for so long and through so many challenges.

Someday we will return to say good-bye to her, and that will be a difficult day as well. I understand grief in a deeper way now because of her. I hope I have learned to be as honest and real in my grief as she was on the day my grandfather was buried.

What Is Grief?

Anyone who suffers a loss will experience grief. The illustration above gives a glimpse into the uniqueness and intensity of grief. If asked to define grief, you probably would describe it as the emotion and pain that come with a loss. But grief is more than the emotional dimension of loss. It has to do not only with feelings—such as anger, guilt or sadness—but also with how the loss affects us socially, psychologically, behaviorally and spiritually. Grief can be described in a number of ways.

The Response to Loss

When we suffer loss, we experience grief. As we saw in chapter 1, loss initiates grief. Grief is how we react to the loss both internally (psychologically, spiritually) and externally (socially, behaviorally). It is an intense period of time filled with pain, emotion, challenges and more.

Grieving is a normal response to loss. It is neither a sickness nor a mental disorder nor in any way an "abnormal" condition. While grieving, we can feel as if we are depressed, "going crazy" or "out of control," but in reality, these feelings are a very normal response to loss. In one sense, "going crazy" is normal in times of grief. Sadly, many people, indeed many Christians, can have a hard time with this. We somehow think that we are immune to grief or are above reacting to loss like others. But in all truthfulness, the Bible is filled with depictions of intensely emotional, "normal" responses to loss.[1] As one expert has said, "Grief is a sign of health itself, a whole and natural gesture of love."[2]

Intensity

The stronger our attachment to the person who dies, the more intense our grief will be. As relationships with people grow and develop over time, our attachment to those people grows. The bonds of love, care, affection and protection bind us together as husband and wife, parent and child, as friends and as family. This is good, but when death ends the relationship our attachment is severed, and the loss of that relationship becomes a source of intense pain.

As seen in the opening story about my grandparents, the intensity of our loss can be overwhelming both physically and emotionally. This intensity will vary from person to person, depending on the circumstances and the depth of relationship the bereaved had with the deceased. However, this intensity should not be viewed as "abnormal" or "out of control." It is a normal response to loss, and it should be understood and respected. Facing the death over time generally brings a lessening of the intensity of grief, but it must be noted that people may experience strong reactions of grief for years after a death.

Grief Work

Psychiatrist Erich Lindemann used the term "grief work" in 1944 to describe tasks that he believed must be successfully completed in order to resolve grief. He coined the term to describe the energy that grief exacts from us physically and emotionally, similar to the physical labor needed to clean a house or mow a lawn. The term also indicates that there is some measure of effort expended by the one grieving in order to move through grief. In other words, grief is work and takes work on our part to resolve it. Psychologist Robert Neimeyer adds, "Grieving is something we do, not something that is done to us."[3]

Uniqueness

As I read Hope Edelman's book *Letters from Motherless Daughters*, I was struck by the radically different stories of women, young and old, who have lost their mothers.[4] Though there are some similarities, every one of them is a unique loss because every mother-daughter relationship is unique. Moreover, every family member's response to the same mother's death is unique. All too often, however, this is not the way death is viewed. In this instance, people might tend to view the death of a mother as the same across the board. We can hear it in the comment, "I know just how you feel; I lost my mother also." Yet it was *your* mother and *your* relationship that only *you* had with her that was lost, not someone else's.

Hopefully, as you read this book, you will come to understand and be comforted, to some degree, by the fact that your loss is unique to you and so is your grief. Do not allow others to minimize your loss by making broad comparisons or generalizations with what they have experienced. Instead, apply what you can learn from other people's situations and appreciate their empathy, but do it in a way that recognizes and maintains the unique relationship that you had with the deceased. It is your relationship with her that should influence your response to her death. You know how she lived, what she liked or didn't like, her character traits, her thinking and opinions, and this is what is unique to your relationship and that which determines your unique response to her death.

Purpose

"What could possibly be the purpose of grief?" we may ask. Grief serves to help us accept the loss, painful reality though it is. The simple fact is that when a person dies, she is gone. Nonetheless, we go through quite a painful process of accepting and adapting to life without that person. Grief is wrapped up in this process of putting our lives back together following a loss. If we stop somewhere in this process, we will not fully face the reality of the loss.

Psychologist Therese Rando says,

> If you fail to adapt following a major loss, if you don't accommodate to the change but persist as if the world is the same when it isn't, then you are not responding to reality, and this is quite unhealthy. The therapeutic purpose of grief and mourning is to get you to the point where you can live with the loss healthily, after having made the necessary changes to do so."[5]

Beginning

Grief is the beginning part of the process of mourning. If we consider the analogy of riding a bicycle, we might describe grief as the first ten miles of a hundred-mile bike ride. I realize that the prospect of grief taking so long can be somewhat challenging, but this is largely due to the fact that our "quick fix" society does not have an accurate idea of the true nature of mourning. (See chapter 3.)

The Affect of Grief

This section describes in greater detail what we experience, both internally and externally, while grieving. If you are now grieving a loss, you will probably identify with this section the most because it describes our affective response—the intense feelings, emotions and thinking patterns of grief. The categories below describe normal grief behaviors that we experience when we have had a loss.[6]

Psychological

Sadness
Fear
Anxiety
Anger
Guilt
Self-reproach
Loneliness
Fatigue
Helplessness
Shock
Yearning
Emancipation (from a difficult relationship or the long process of death)
Relief
Joy or happiness
Numbness
Disbelief
Confusion
Preoccupation
A sense of presence of the deceased
Hallucinatory experiences

Physical

Hollowness in the stomach
A lump in the throat
Tightness in the chest
Aching arms
Oversensitivity to noise
Shortness of breath
Lack of energy
A sense of depersonalization
Muscle weakness
Dry mouth
Loss of coordination
Upset stomach
Sleep difficulties
Fatigue
Nervousness
Dizziness
Apathy
Crying
Sighing
Absentmindedness

Social

Withdrawal
Difficulty with interpersonal relationships
Problems functioning on the job or in a group
Restlessness
Loss of interest in activities
Irritated by others
Bored
Lack of motivation
Preoccupied
Isolated

Spiritual

Searching for a sense of meaning
Hostility toward God
Inadequacy of value system
Questioning God

Grief and Time

How long does grief last? It has no set timetable. Our society is confused about this, with some contending that grieving should last a couple of weeks, or maybe six months to a year; however, this simply is not the case. Generally, grief is more intense during the early days and months following a death, but this is not always true. For instance, someone who refuses to deal with the death of a loved one will likely experience grief later on, perhaps as intensely as if it had just happened. Over time grief will tend to become less intense; but at certain times, such as the anniversary of the death, strong feelings and reactions may resurface for a period of time.

Although grief does not have an exact timetable, it will help to know that we usually experience it in a number of ways over time. It is unique to each person and is not experienced in a linear progression from one way to the next. Those who grieve may go back and forth between periods of response as they try to live daily and come to terms with the loss of a loved one. These periods of response could be summarized as initial, connecting and adapting.

Initial. At the very beginning, there is a refusal to engage or an inability to engage the loss. We have learned of the death and cannot comprehend it. It is the shock, panic, disbelief, confusion, numbness and inability to make sense of the death that immediately besets us. It is the reaction, "I can't believe it" or "No, no, no...it can't be true...I saw her only yesterday." When the shock begins to wear off, denial can then set in to buffer our inability to cope with the full and intense reality of the death. Denial must not be perceived as bad or wrong, but more like the way our mind structures a path for us to take in order to deal with the loss.

Connecting. This period of response occurs as we start to gradually absorb the full impact of the loss. By this time we have recognized and admitted that the loss has occurred and the shock is beginning to wear off. We begin to fully experience the effects of grief that were listed earlier (psychologically, physically, socially, spiritually).

Adapting. When grief becomes more manageable or the intensity gradually begins to decline, we are responding in more accommodating ways towards the loss. We can still be in the process of mourning, but the intense feelings are diminishing little by little. We hold on to the memories of our loved one, but we are beginning to look at life in a changed way. Little by little our energy returns, and our concentration and functioning improve. We begin to reestablish emotional control, and our sleeping and eating habits begin to return to normal. We are starting to reinvest in life again. We now know that we will survive, but we are a different person because of the loss.

Spiritual Notes

The Emotions of Grief

Christians and non-Christians alike feel the effects of grief. Christians will experience anger, sadness, guilt, shock, numbness and more—we are not somehow impervious to grief (see John 11:35, Philippians 2:27 and Acts 8:2 for some examples). The expression of intense emotions caused by grief is usually a challenge, not only for those who grieve, but also for those around them. We must remember that behavior that seems "abnormal" or "over the line" may in fact be very normal in grief. We must learn to respond to such expressions of grief in a spiritual way, with patience and compassion and under-standing. Listed below are two typical emotions for us to be aware of so that we do not overreact to those in mourning, making grief more difficult for those going through it.

Anger

Anger should be expected in grief. It is a natural response to the loss of anyone or anything that is valuable to us. As a Christian, we may find it hard to handle the raw anger vented by a grieving person (Ruth 1:20–21, John 11:32–35). We may feel even more strange if we ourselves are the ones doing the venting. In the course of grieving, anger may be expressed toward others or ourselves, or it might be suppressed by telling ourselves that we should not be angry. There are many reasons people are angry when a death has occurred, and a few of them are listed below:

- Being left as a survivor
- Remembering things the deceased did or did not do
- Dealing with the circumstances of the death, such as at the hands of a drunk driver
- Not agreeing with God's role—what he did or didn't do for the deceased
- Being unable to have personally prevented the death
- Being aware of others' possible responsibility in the death, such as the doctor who operated

How do we deal with the anger of Christians who are grieving? Here are some helpful suggestions:

- Don't overreact, but listen to them. Obviously, if they are intent on hurting themselves, others or even property, then you need to seek immediate help and intervention from their doctor, a hospital or even the police (911 in most areas).

• Don't quickly try to answer, correct or discipline those who are expressing anger as part of their grief. This can hurt your ability to be a comfort and a resource to them. Be patient and gentle. Give them the time and opportunity to express their feelings.

• Do not quickly judge their behavior as sin. Remember that anger in grief is normal and that they are probably responding normally to loss. Sinful anger is generally present when our response is driven by our own selfish desires (James 1:14). However, anger in grief is driven by loss. In other words, the catalyst to anger in grief is predicated by an external source (loss) rather than an internal source (desire). Thus we need to be cautious in determining what kind of anger is occurring. Angry responses out of desire—a fit of rage when I do not get a parking space—need to be confronted as sin and dealt with as such. Angry responses that come from loss need to be approached with wisdom, compassion and patience.

• Allow them to express their anger in a healthy way (such as crying, venting, working, exercising) or assist them in finding an appropriate expression. One ground rule is that they cannot hurt themselves, others or property.

• Reassure them that they can talk to God. You may be uncomfortable with a grieving person expressing anger at God, but God isn't. He knows the depth of loss that we suffer and wants us to talk with him about it—even if we do it with more intense emotion than we ever have before. Just read the Psalms and see how honest David was with God when he was working through grief and other emotions.

• Hang in there with people. Anger does not go away in a few days or after an episode or two.

As a concluding word of caution, if we are immature in the way we handle the anger of those who are grieving, we can do them considerable harm. We can cause the bereaved to "clam up" and not be open about their real feelings. Eventually this can lead them to turn their anger inward and to harm themselves by growing bitter, resentful or depressed or even to explode at some point over stored-up rage. Also, not allowing them the opportunity to express their anger can push them away from those who could help them work through their anger. It can also signal to them that they are "wrong" in expressing their anger—and if *fellow Christians* think they are wrong, then certainly God must view them as being wrong as well. This obviously could push them in a direction away from God and cause them not to lay their feelings, questions and requests before him—the exact opposite of what God desires.

Guilt

Guilt may surface after a death in many different ways:

• Being the one who lived while the other person died

• Feeling as if we might have contributed to the death in some way

• Focusing on the "if onlys," the "should (or shouldn't) haves" and the "why dids or did nots"

- Thinking that the death occurred because of something we did or some sin we committed
- Feeling better or not feeling as bad about the death anymore
- Feeling relief that the person is dead

In death Christians can feel any of the types of guilt listed above. We can feel that there are things we should have said or done or things we wished we hadn't said or done. This is generally the case and is very normal after a death. Eventually (and immediately after the death may not be the best time) we need to look at the truth about the deceased and the relationship we had with her in order to accurately assess our guilty thinking. Our tendency, especially near the time of death, can be to idealize our relationship with the deceased; but later, greater honesty will be required. We will need to be honest about the true nature of our relationship: the positive and negative aspects, the good and the bad, the up side and the down side. (Additionally, to give us a more accurate picture, the facts surrounding the death may need to be investigated in certain situations such as automobile accidents or medical circumstances). Answers are not always readily available and must be pursued.

This process of evaluating the relationship may reveal situations that were negative to the point of unhealthiness, neglect or even abuse. It may surface guilt in a more complex way for the bereaved. If we are in this situation, we may experience guilt for feeling relieved that the person who abused us is dead. The inquiry into and examination of the relationship can help us begin to address issues that could complicate our journey through mourning. These types of situations require much sensitivity since they can be very difficult to deal with. Traumatic events have often been part of past relationships, and more harm can be done when things are handled in an immature way. Professional help may be required especially when dealing with issues such as abuse.

This process may take some time, investigation, openness and help from others to talk about what the relationship was really like. However, in doing so, it gives God the opportunity to challenge and correct our thinking, perceptions and feelings with the truth of his word, and to help us come to terms with whether the guilt is justifiable or not. In other words, we must ultimately figure out what is false or true about our thinking.

There may be occasions when someone is legitimately guilty of something toward the person who died. If you are struggling with this type of guilt, I would advise you to get help and advice from mature spiritual people who can talk through and examine your situation and help you determine what course of action you need to take. In the end, acknowledging your mistakes and errors, and making restitution when possible may be the only way of dealing with your guilt, allowing you to emotionally accept forgiveness for yourself (or from others). Whether the guilt is legitimate or not, you need to remember that for the Christian, God's word says that he is merciful and extends forgiveness when we ask for it, regardless of the magnitude of the sin or the consequences.

The Intensity of Grief

Grief will be intense for the Christian just as it is for anyone else. However, a loss that might particularly increase the intensity of grief for a Christian is the death of someone who is not a Christian. The intensity of our grief can be greater when we consider the concept of eternity and the Biblical view of the final destiny of people outside of God's plan. For instance, if we believe that the Bible teaches about two eternal destinies, "heaven" and "hell," then the death of a non-Christian friend or family member could cause us considerably more grief if we believed their destiny was "hell" rather than "heaven." Spiritually, we may view the death with a greater sense of tragedy and hopelessness than others do because of the eternal ramifications. In other words, our grief may be more intense if we feel that the deceased did not have a relationship with God and was "lost"—lost because we have lost the person physically (in this life) and eternally (in the next life) because of no hope of reunion. In my experience, Christians need to consider this as a factor regarding the intensity of their own grief in the loss of a person who is not a Christian. Also, it should help us to be more aware and sensitive to others in the loss of their non-Christian friends and family.

Responding to the Intensity of Grief

It should go without saying that to stand and face the intensity of grief, we need to continue to pray and read the Bible, and stay close to other Christians. However, it is just as important to work through things with God. Grief, if we choose to allow it to, can push us away from God. We can harden our hearts and move away from him or we can choose to stay and wrestle it out. Unfortunately, some will let loss harden their hearts. The pain and grief of the loss will cause them to ask questions that at the moment may not be answered. Or they will walk away from God's presence and seek solace in other places. In such cases, we can only hope their hearts will become open to approaching God at some future time.

God wants us to hang in there and work through our painful feelings with him. We find this in many places in the Bible, though the story of Job is probably the most prominent one. After the death of his children, the loss of his wealth, the loss of support from his spiritual partner (as his wife advised him to curse God and die) and then the loss of his own health, Job stayed with God and sought answers. He looked for reasons, and even demanded a debate with God (Job 13:3). In the midst of great suffering and the insensitive counsel of friends, he did not quit looking for answers and searching for meaning (Job 13:15). He chose to stay and wrestle.

Job's example is echoed in the lives of people like Jesus, the apostle Paul, Mary the mother of Jesus, David, Elisha, Hezekiah and others, who, having experienced loss, chose to stay close to God and other spiritual men and women. In the midst of their grief, they prayed, sought comfort in the Scriptures, wept, retreated (both alone and with others), wrote out their pain (Lamentations and Psalms), sang, served others, worked and waited. They stayed with whatever strength they could muster and with the belief expressed by Paul, "I know whom I have believed, and am convinced that he is able to guard what I have entrusted to him" (2 Timothy 1:12). They were willing to walk through the pain and the anguish with God, rather than without him. They were not superheroes, but simply men and women who were convinced that God could help them see their way through the "valley of the shadow of death" (see Psalm 23 and Hebrews 11:37–38).

We need to choose to work through things with God, even if we are wrestling with the spiritual destiny of our loved ones or if death has shaken us to the point of questioning our beliefs. Knowing that intense grief is normal and that it creates a spiritual upheaval for everyone (Acts 9:39) helps us to believe that we can survive and get through it. It may take some time and we need to be patient. But we have to hold on to scriptures like John 6:68, in which Peter says, in the midst of a spiritual crisis, "Lord, to whom shall we go? You have the words of eternal life."

Give the Bereaved Time

Hopefully by now, we know that grief requires time. Our temptation may be to bring grief under control quickly and get things "resolved." I hope we will fight this notion. People who are grieving need time and a "wide berth" of love, gentleness, kindness, grace, patience (which sound a lot like the gifts of the Spirit found in Galatians 5:22–23) in order to live through their loss. You will have a better understanding of this when you finish chapter 3 on mourning. So for now, give the griever, whether yourself or someone else, time to work through the grieving process.

Grief is a normal reaction to loss. It is probably the part of the process of mourning with which we identify most, due to its intense effects. Grief—and the duration of grief—is unique to each person. Spiritually, as well as in every other way, we can live through grief. It is not easy, but God is there to walk with us. If we stay close to him, he will eventually see us through it.

I wanted to be strong when my husband died. I did not want my boys to see me grieving because I thought that would make it more difficult for them. Hence, they followed my lead. Neither of them would let himself show emotion because, after all, Mom wasn't crying. We could have helped each other so much if we had taken time to sit down and talk and cry together.

—Joyce

3
Mourning

Penny is a friend of our family whom we met while her father was dying of cancer. He had been fighting it for a number of years, and his battle dominated the family picture in such a way as to overshadow everything else. He was a loving husband and a wonderful friend, and for Penny he was the perfect dad.

His death a number of years ago left a huge hole in Penny's life. Mourning the loss has been a long and challenging trial. She spent the early years in disbelief, having a hard time realizing that he was gone for good. Tremendous sadness began to fill the void that formerly had been filled with his love and encouragement.

The death of Penny's father also led to the emotional disintegration of her family. They had a tough time pulling together, and in the end, they separated to try to deal with their grief individually. Work became difficult for Penny. She could not concentrate and began to feel as if there was something physically wrong with her. Socially, while she had friends, she had no one close enough to cling to for real help and support. Spiritually, she struggled. Before her father's death, Penny's walk with God was an area of her life that she didn't question much; now she had many questions, but no answers. She did not want to blame God, so instead, she chose to stuff the thoughts and feelings and keep moving, hoping somehow this would all work out in time.

Time, however, did not magically heal her heart. Penny has come to understand that mourning does not end after a few months or years; rather, it has become an ongoing part of her life. She is learning to live with it. She has had to reexamine old expectations of her father's presence in her life and form new expectations. She has started to view herself more as her own person, not just her father's daughter. With her family she is learning to be responsible for her life and not take on the role of being the strong one who holds the whole family together. She is continuing to work at new relationships and is trying to be open and honest about her life, even when others do not understand the impact of this death on her. Spiritually, Penny is wrestling for a new faith, a faith that is hers, not her father's. This continues to take time. Years have come and gone. She misses her dad no less today than on the day he died—some days even more. In the end, if she continues to live and learn, she will make it. And she will be able to share with others what it really means to mourn.

Some Myths About Mourning

Before looking at what mourning is, consider the following common misunderstandings and myths:

1. Grief and mourning always decline in a steadily decreasing fashion over time.

2. All losses prompt the same type of mourning.

3. Intensity and length of mourning are a testimony to love for the deceased.

4. Losing someone to a sudden, unexpected death is the same as losing someone to an anticipated death.

5. Mourning is finished in a year.

6. To be healthy after the death of a loved one, the mourner must put that person out of mind.

7. Bereaved individuals need only to express their feelings in order to resolve their mourning.

8. It is better to tell people to "Be brave" and "Keep a stiff upper lip" because then they will not have to experience as much pain.

9. Parents usually divorce after a child dies.

10. You can find ways to avoid the pain of your grief and still resolve it successfully.[1]

Have you ever heard anyone express thoughts like these? Have you ever thought or said any of them yourself? We will never successfully resolve our grief—or be in a position to help others through this difficult process—until we start to understand what the process of mourning is really all about.

What Is Mourning?

The story that opens this chapter is about mourning. We have already learned that loss initiates grief and that grief is the beginning of the journey we call mourning. One author defines the journey of mourning this way:

> The term "mourning" indicates the processes of coping with loss and grief, and thus the attempt to manage those experiences or learn to live with them by incorporating them into ongoing living.[2]

Simply put, mourning is *living with our bereavement.* When we experience loss, we must then learn to live life in a new and different way. We need to learn to live without the person we lost, while at the same time, continuing to face life's daily routines and experiences. This is the mourning process. You may be feeling that you have never heard mourning characterized or described in this way, and you are probably right. Many of us in Western culture have not been taught much about mourning, other than the notion that it is the outward display of emotion at a funeral or the public acknowledgment of a death in some way. These are small parts of mourning, but we need a more accurate view of this process that each of us will surely experience.

Today, there is a good deal of change and evolution in our understanding of mourning as experts in the field reexamine and redefine this important process. Why? The simple answer is that our society has radically changed its view of death in the last 150 years. We have moved from a time when death was an ever-present part of each person's life experience (prior to the 1900s) to an age in which society denies and avoids the subject of death at all costs. As a result, we have had to *rediscover* how to deal with death. To understand this better, let's look at a little history of the study of grief and mourning. This will give us some background on mourning that will eventually help us formulate the kind of healthy perspective that we as Christians need to have.

A Brief History

Early study and research regarding mourning dwelt more on observable symptoms: emotions, behaviors and physical signs. Researchers such as Freud, Lindemann, Bowlby and

Engel contributed much to our understanding of how grief affects us psychologically, physically, socially and behaviorally. In 1969 Dr. Elizabeth Kubler-Ross, a Swiss-American psychiatrist, published her book *On Death and Dying*, setting forth a theoretical, stage-based model of reactions experienced by people who were dying.[3] She has since become the most widely read author on this topic in the world. Her book has been published in nearly as many languages as the Bible, and her understanding of grief continues to be the most popular and influential theory, especially in the United States.

Simply put, Dr. Kubler-Ross observed that most people faced with death move through five stages of grief:

1. Denial

2. Anger

3. Bargaining

4. Depression

5. Acceptance

However, Kubler-Ross's work has often been misapplied. Those who used her five-stage linear model found it woefully inadequate for understanding and assisting those in mourning. Today, even though the limitations of her work have been identified, many people still erroneously hold to Kubler-Ross's five stages as the best way to describe grief.

Beginning in the early 1970s, further research and study began to produce various models of mourning that were more in keeping with the mourning experience. Psychiatrists John Bowlby and Colin Murray Parkes were among the pioneers. They described mourning as four phases that must be traversed before resolution will occur:

1. Shock and numbness

2. Yearning and searching

3. Disorganization and despair

4. Reorganization[4]

Later on, William Worden described mourning as a set of interrelated tasks to complete before resolution. He used the term "tasks" because he felt that certain work needed to be completed by the mourner in order to properly work through the loss. His four tasks are

1. To accept the reality of the loss

2. To work through to the pain of grief

3. To adjust to an environment in which the deceased is missing

4. To emotionally relocate the deceased and move on with life[5]

Psychologist Therese Rando went on to describe mourning as a series of processes that we work through. She preferred the term "processes" to convey the idea that we can go back and forth among them (not a linear progression) and can evaluate as we go. She believes that describing mourning as a series of processes keeps the emphasis on understanding and helping the mourner, rather than on the completion of tasks. According to Rando, all of six processes must be completed to have healthy mourning:

1. Recognize the loss—acknowledge and understand the death.

2. React to the separation—experience the pain of the loss; feel, identify, accept and give expression to all the

psychological reactions to the loss; and identify and mourn secondary losses.

3. Recollect and re-experience the deceased and the relationship—review and remember realistically; revive and re-experience one's feelings.

4. Relinquish old attachments to the deceased and the old assumptive world (the way we viewed and lived in the world prior to the loss).

5. Readjust to move adaptively into the "new" world without forgetting the old—revise the assumptive world, develop a new relationship with the deceased, adopt new ways of being in the world, and form a new identity.

6. Reinvest (in a "new" life without the deceased).[6]

Hopefully you have found it helpful to briefly survey some of the ways mourning has been viewed and worked with in the past several decades. Obviously this is a simplification of years of study, research and "hands on" experience by those who work with the bereaved. To summarize, recent clinical and theoretical studies of grieving have yielded some important insights into the mourning process:

- The need to work through mourning over time

- The patterns and ways of coping

- The importance of "working" through and "processing" grief

- The normalcy of mourning, adapted to over time

- The value of understanding the bereaved throughout the whole context of mourning

Keys to Understanding Mourning

As Christians, how do we find our way through the myriad of books, people, models and theories in order to get a handle on the mourning process? Keeping it simple, the approach to mourning that I would suggest is to know about the bereaved and to know the journey of bereavement.

Know About the Bereaved

It is essential to know about the bereaved person (personality, emotional make-up, response to stressful situations, etc.) so we can better understand his (or our) unique mourning experience. The better informed helpers are, the better they will be able to help and support their friends or family members.

Every person who mourns is unique. Proverbs says, "Each heart knows its own bitterness" (Proverbs 14:10). Perhaps the best way to illustrate this is to provide a list of questions to help us think about bereaved people in a deeper way. As a framework for asking these questions, consider how the loss may be affecting the person psychologically, socially, physically and spiritually.

Psychologically

1. How is he handling the death?

2. What type of personality does he have?

3. Is he an overly emotional person by nature?

4. How does he typically cope with difficult situations?

5. Does he have problems with emotions such as anger, depression, fear or low self-esteem?

6. Does he have any prior psychological history?

Socially

1. Has she suffered the loss of other people? Who were they? How long ago?

2. What type of social circle does she have? Is it support-ive or not?

3. Is she an active or an isolated person?

4. What is her family or extended family like socially?

5. Have there been any problems with family relation-ships historically?

6. How do they all communicate?

7. What is her cultural background? Are there any cus-toms or traditions that are important to recognize or consider?[7]

Physically

1. Is the death affecting him physically?

2. Does he have any physical challenges or prior health issues?

3. Does he exercise regularly?

4. How does he cope with stress physically?

5. How is he doing presently with sleeping, eating and getting exercise or rest?

Spiritually

1. What does this loss mean to her?

2. What was her relationship like with the deceased?

3. How was she doing spiritually before the death?

4. Does she have questions of "lost or saved" about the deceased?

5. Is there any unfinished business with the deceased that has suddenly emerged or any past situations that were not resolved?

6. Does this death present any spiritual dilemmas for her?

7. Will this death present any opportunity for growth for her?

8. What type of relationships does she have with other Christians?

9. What changes will this death bring about in her life?

10. How does she typically cope with crisis spiritually?

As you can see by asking some questions, it helps us to think more deeply about those who are bereaved. It causes us to "in humility consider others" (Philippians 2:3) and to think about them in a more meditative way, beyond the level of casual friendship. It asks us to consider walking with them through their loss and understanding their point of view, rather than assuming a predetermined set of criteria that they must live up to. If we are the ones who are bereaved, these questions help us understand why we are responding in certain ways. Having this view of a bereaved person will help us to remember that "who they are" is as significant as "what they are going through."

The more in touch we are with "who the bereaved are" psychologically, socially, physically and spiritually, the better situated we will be to understand and to help. In general everyone requires some help in living through mourning. However, our help becomes more focused when we know more than just how they are doing emotionally. For instance, if I knew that the person struggled with depression, then I might make sure that I stayed in closer contact with him. If the person was not doing well spiritually prior to a death, then I would expect him to probably do worse following a death. As a result of knowing this, I can gear my help more toward loving, serving and comforting him rather than having unrealistic expectations for him. By knowing about the bereaved person, we can make better decisions about how to respond to his unique circumstances.

Know the Journey of Bereavement

The journey of bereavement can best be described as a process of change over time. I have chosen to break this process down into three areas or periods of time that are part of the mourning process. These periods are neither set in stone nor are they necessarily linear progressions that follow one after the other. They describe tendencies that have some progression to them; however, they may emerge in different ways at any time and place during the years in which mourning is prevalent.

Initial Loss and Grief

The early period of mourning is the initial, intense period of loss and grief. It encompasses the death, dealing with the death and eventually acknowledging the death. As bereaved people, we will be dealing with extreme feelings and emotions, eventually embracing the pain they bring. This time usually includes the early public acknowledgments of the death such as the wake, funeral and/or memorial service. During this time, our minds will protect us through denial, insulating us from the immediate pain and change that death has now brought into our world. However at some point, reality sets in and as it does, the pain of loss increases.

Eventually grief will subside somewhat, not dominating our thoughts or emotions as strongly as in the beginning. We will continue to live our lives, and as we do, we will begin to adapt to the loss.

Times of Change and Decision

As we move away from the time of death, we face a new reality. We come to realize life has changed—it will not be the same as before. For instance, the wife of the deceased may have become a widow and at the same time a single mother. Roles, social context and family structure may all have changed in a matter of moments. As the period of acute grief begins to abate, these changes will become more and more apparent. Some changes will be associated more with the death (like cleaning out the deceased's closet, changing the answering machine recording, paying the bills), while others will have to do more with creating a new life (like taking up a new hobby, finding a job, learning to cook, going on a trip or repainting the house).

With these changes will come some unique decisions, such as how to deal with our relationship to the deceased or how we choose to remember the deceased. Some decisions will be more practical, such as selling a car, moving to a smaller house or apartment and selling or throwing away items that belonged to the one who died. Other decisions concern developing a new identity or family role. One decision may be that we must now make decisions, which may be new for some of us. All of these contribute to the process of change. Since loss has altered our world, we must now face the new reality that has come as a result.

Living with the Loss

Mourning is learning to live with bereavement. There is not a set time in which mourning runs its course. Living with the loss is an ongoing process through life. This process can mean (1) learning new roles or a new identity, (2) adjusting to or creating a new family structure or set of relationships, or (3) changing towns, jobs, dreams or goals. In time, living with the loss will become more manageable (unless other factors complicate it), but mourning can continue for years—even a lifetime. While in mourning, we will go back and forth between dealing with the loss and putting our lives back together. Our ability to cope with our changed world will be challenged time and again, but we will continue to adapt and accommodate to the loss. Slowly, though we are forever changed by the loss, we will "relearn" the world and live a new life without our loved one.

During this time there will be opportunities for new beginnings. The search for meaning can be an ongoing process. Many will find answers that will satisfy and sustain them while for others it may be a journey that lasts for years to come. Some will find new meaning in life that would never have occurred without having experienced the loss. They will experience growth and transformation following a death, such as becoming more devoted Christians, becoming more loving people or developing stronger character. They may gain a better perspective on life and relationships, all as a result of the loss. In summary, mourning can be described as a process initiated by loss and grief that brings life-changes and decisions. It is learning to live with our loss over time.

Spiritual Notes

The Search for Meaning

One of the greatest challenges found in mourning is searching for meaning in the death and asking the question "Why?" "Why did my child die?" "Why did this happen?" "Why now?" I have talked with many people whose stories of loss left me sitting there without an immediate answer. On the other hand, I do believe that knowing God and having a Biblical understanding can provide some clues about God's purposes for suffering that we can trust and be comforted by. In other words, I do not believe there is one exact answer or meaning to all the losses in our lives; rather, a number of factors about which the Bible speaks can combine to speak to our situation. The answers we find may run contrary to what we want, feel or think. But in time, from the numerous teachings and examples of suffering found in the Bible, each of us can— with God's guidance and in his time—understand something about the meaning of the loss for us personally.

For some deaths this may not be such a large issue. For instance, we may have had a grandparent who lived to an old age. We may also know that he was neither open to learning about God nor desirous of having a relationship with him. When he died at the age of eighty-two, knowing some of the choices he had made for his life mitigated our search for meaning in his death.

For those who struggle with asking "Why?" and find that looking in your Bible is not helping, I would encourage you to ask for assistance from others and to keep trying. Early in the grief process it is more difficult to think through such things, but as time passes, hopefully you will be in a better position to deal with your questions. Also, as you search for answers to these difficult questions, I would suggest that you put yourself in a safe, supportive environment of Christian help. Hang in there—don't quit! Remember that in "the valley of the shadow of death" God always walks with us and remains our ultimate hope (see Psalm 23).

Often people who suffer loss are reminded of the fleeting nature of life, and the reality of death all around us. We must not forget that Christianity provides powerful and unique answers to these "big" questions about life and death.

> The faith of the New Testament—and it can be our faith—is that death and the deadly threats of evil are swallowed up in victory, that amid difficulties we are kept in God's boundless and invincible love, and that we can trust his good will ultimately to prevail.[8]

In chapter 4, I have written on a number of topics that present God's perspective and teaching about life and death that should comfort and encourage you and aid in your Bible study. Hopefully they will lead you to a more informed view about life and suffering. Below I have listed a number of views of suffering along with scriptures (which I will abbreviate for space). These views are based on the premise that suffering is better understood by the Christian when looking at the example of Jesus' suffering in his life and death. The cross teaches us that suffering can be understood, and that even in the midst of suffering the Christian finds real meaning and real comfort.

Views of Suffering in the New Testament

- *Our Connection with Christ's suffering* – suggests that suffering is not some strange thing happening to us, but parallels the suffering of Christ and gives us meaning and insight into our own suffering.

  1 Peter 4:12–19

  2 Corinthians 1:5, 4:7–10

  Philippians 2:1–11

- *Increases our dependence on God and not on ourselves* – suffering reminds us of the temporary and fragile nature of worldly supports and foundations and of our utter need to depend on God.

  2 Corinthians 1:3–11, 12:7–9

  Psalm 68:19

- *Proves and refines* – suffering causes us to test and prove our faith and awakens our ability to face, endure and overcome challenges.

  Hebrews 2:10; 10:32, 36; 12:1–2

  Revelation 2:2–3, 19; 14:12

  Mark 13:13

  Romans 5:3–4, 12:12

Note: This material is adapted from Erhard S. Gerstenberger and Wolfgang Schrange, *Suffering*, trans. John C. Steely (Nashville: Abington, 1977), 205–242.

James 5:11

2 Timothy 2:11–13

- *Elicits hope* – in the midst of great suffering rises the need for hope.

  Romans 4:17; 5:1–5,

  2 Corinthians 4:13–18

  1 Peter 1:3–9

  Job 13:14–15

- *Causes others to see Jesus* – suffering brings the testimony of Jesus to the world around us.

  Mark 15:39

  Acts 5:41, 11:9, 16:25–34

  Ephesians 3:7–13

  2 Timothy 2:8–10

- *Points us heavenward* – only the eternal relationship with God provides real comfort in life and death.

  Romans 8:18

  2 Corinthians 5:1–5

  Revelation 21:1–4

  1 Peter 1:6, 13

Spiritual Health Affects Mourning

Mourning will be different for every Christian. What makes it unique is not just our unique loss and our unique life and personality, but also our unique relationship with God. How we are doing spiritually can directly affect how we mourn. If a person has a deep relationship with God, chances are he will weather the storm of grief and mourning better than someone who has a shallow or superficial one. A Christian with cancer once told me that upon sharing his prognosis with other Christians, the Christians who had a deeper relationship with God received the news far better than did those who were just beginning their spiritual walk with God. However, even strong, mature Christians can have a difficult time with losses, especially the death of a child or a sudden and violent death of a loved one. Paul describes the depth of pain that even the strong can experience in the middle of suffering when he writes,

> We do not want you to be uninformed, brothers, about the hardships we suffered in the province of Asia. We were under great pressure, far beyond our ability to endure, so that we despaired even of life. (2 Corinthians 1:8)

If the great apostle Paul could feel overwhelmed spiritually, imagine how a young or weak Christian whose faith may be fragile might struggle spiritually with a sudden or traumatic loss.

It is important to consider how any Christian is doing spiritually in the face of loss. But we should especially consider the spiritually younger or weaker Christians as Paul did when he enjoined the disciples in Galatia to "carry each other's burdens" (Galatians 6:2). We can help them until they are strong enough to carry their own load. "Considering" means that we must take care to deal with people where they are spiritually, not where we might *want* them to be. The initial period of grief is not the time to expect them to do better spiritually than prior to the death. However, with support, encouragement, help, prayer and some time-appropriate reconstruction, their spiritual roots can grow stronger and eventually help them to make it through their mourning.

Time

Giving time to people in mourning can be a spiritual challenge. As Christians, we may feel the need to resolve things quickly. For instance, with sin, we expect repentance, change and commitment to doing right, right now! But mourning is not sin, and neither society nor we should have the expectation that others "hurry up and get over it." Patience is required. In the midst of difficult times the Bible continually urges us to persevere, to endure and to have hope—all of which call upon us to bear each other's burdens, even when it is for a long time. It may be harder for us to do, but this is the right way to serve the bereaved Christian. We must affirm that the Bible teaches us to bear with people in difficult times and accept the natural response of humans to mourn as God created us to do.

Use of Terms

I believe semantics regarding mourning are important. The use of words such as "closure," "healing," "recovery" need to be considered and used in appropriate ways. For instance, some people who work in the field of grief and mourning do not choose to use the word "recovery" because of certain connotations.

First, it indicates that a person was once normal and then got sick and then was given something for it and then "recovered" (returned to normal). The use of this term can suggest that once the remedy was applied that this process took only a certain amount of time. However, experiencing a death is not like dealing with a sickness. The view that there is a specific time when people return to normal, are healed, find closure and complete resolution—as suggested by the word "recover"—can be misleading. After a death, our lives will never be the same as they were before. We will not at some point return to a "normal" state because the old normal is gone. The same could be said of healing and closure. We may feel the pain of loss and not reach complete closure on some issues for the rest of our lives.

Second, use of the word "recovery" can imply that mourning is something bad that has happened. Mourning is a hard and painful part of life, but at the same time it is not all "bad." God has created us such that we are capable of growing through loss, grief and mourning. He knew that, as finite creatures, we would experience loss over and over again. Many people have been changed into stronger, more compassionate, spiritual people due to loss. Paul indicated this when he wrote, "We are hard pressed on every side, but not crushed...struck down, but not destroyed" (2 Corinthians 4:8–9). He implies that even under extreme emotional and physical pressure and duress, we are not crushed or destroyed, but can—indeed are created to—endure.

The word Paul uses in Romans 5:3–4 for suffering means "the ability to feel or endure pain and to bear loss, damage or injury." So he says that we can rejoice in our sufferings (bearing of losses) because they are part of producing even greater character and hope (Romans 5:3). Viewing mourning as a natural part of life—one that we learn to live through—allows us to acknowledge progress, growth, functioning and transcendence, rather than anticipating an event from which no good can come.

In the end we need to view the outcome as God does. Jesus declared,

> "I have told you these things, so that in me you may have peace. In this world you will have trouble. But take heart! I have overcome the world." (John 16:33)

Jesus shared this thought with his disciples in preparation for their own mourning of his death. He acknowledges the trouble (the pain and anguish of loss and mourning) and states the fact that they will have it in this world. Yet he encourages them, even in such times of trouble, to take heart—because following him will allow them to overcome and rise above their troubles. Spiritually speaking, God has encouraged us to search for the good in loss. Even though we will experience the difficulty of loss in our days on earth, he has secured our eternal future through Jesus, who gives us peace and the hope of living and growing through mourning, even in this life. Ultimately for the Christian, the most important concern for our mourning is to stay connected to Jesus and the peace and eternal hope of overcoming, rather than seeking to "recover" from it. Let us think through what and how we communicate about mourning so that we can help create an appropriate environment for those who mourn and for those who help those who mourn.

My Story
The Loss of My Father
Mark Buchholz

It has been more than five years since I got the call. It was not "the call" but one almost as bad. It was my mom and dad calling to tell me that Dad had cancer again. I say again because my dad was no stranger to cancer. In 1962 he went in for a routine checkup and they found a small lump on his throat. No big deal. Then the results came back, it was the worst kind of lymphoma. The doctors quickly formulated a plan: massive surgery to remove all the tissue around the affected area and then radiation as a follow-up. I was seven at the time and really didn't know what was going on. All I remember was going to stay with some friends of the family and getting to play with one of my best friends while my dad and mom went away. I didn't think much of it at the time. I do remember seeing my dad after the treatment. He looked bad; they had removed so much tissue and he had the longest scar I had ever seen.

I remember life slowly returning to normal; him throwing the baseball with me and spending time with me again. So this first brush with death was one in which we dodged the bullet. Now we were dancing with the devil a second time.

Dad had angiosarcoma, a rare cancer of the blood vessels. It first appeared right on the top of his head. As before, they plotted a strategy. This time they would follow the same path chosen almost thirty-six years before: surgery to remove the cancer and

68

radiation to follow. This would be the beginning of Dad's three-and-a-half year battle with cancer that would entail three surgeries, three sessions of radiation and months and even years of chemo. My dad was a fighter, and to the very end he pushed through the pain. One of the hardest things was to watch his deterioration.

We took several trips to visit him through these three years, which helped a lot. Near the end I took a special trip separately with each of the kids and finally my wife to say good-bye. Those trips were particularly hard because we knew each was a time to say good-bye. But the talks we had, the times to serve and to reminisce were very special. Each of the children has special memories from those visits with Grandpa. Dad and I would talk about God and pray when we were together; I also would write him and share scriptures with him. He did draw close to God at that time and got some comfort from our times to talk and pray and from reading my letters. I shared with him all that he had meant to me through the years and why he was so special to me. I cried many tears as I wrote those letters, but I think they helped me to get in touch with the loss and prepared me for his leaving this life.

The other aspect that was hard was watching how this affected my mom. She was the primary caretaker through the entire time and was so stretched. She had lost a lot of weight, did not sleep much and was so worried. She and my dad had been married almost sixty years and she was losing the love of her life.

After our last visit, he made the decision to stop his chemo. It was an emotional time, especially for my mom. It meant he was ready to go, but she was not ready for him to go and had to surrender to his choice. I also had made the decision along with my wife to ride in the Pan-Mass Challenge, a two-day, two-hundred mile ride to raise money for the Jimmy Fund, the main charity for one of the best cancer research centers here in Boston. Training for it helped me to work through my upcoming loss and helped Beth and me to stay close. We would pray together as a family often and spoke with my mom and dad continually on the phone.

In spite of all that is going on you cannot put your life on hold so we took the family on a trip to Florida in July, knowing that the time was near and that he may even slip away while we were down there. That Sunday, Dad went to meet God. We continued our trip, and I had some very special times with my brothers and their families before we all went home to bury Dad. We had a graveside service, and because Dad had served in the military in WW II, they had an honor guard and played taps and folded the flag. It was a great memory seeing my dad so honored.

At the memorial, each of his sons shared our special memories. John, one of my special Christian friends from Boston, flew down with his son to be at the service. As I shared about my dad, I was strengthened to see John sitting in the audience.

Beth and I did the ride, and it was one of the hardest things I had ever done. I had thrown my back out a week before, and the pain during the ride was terrible. But I rode to the end, each mile thinking about my dad and the way he endured his pain. When we finally saw the tower at Provincetown in the distance, I wept. I had made it and this was for Dad; it was the beginning of the grief process and healing that God would bring about.

One of my special memories since then was a prayer walk that I had with my friend Charlie on Duxbury beach one morning. He had lost his mom several years before; and as we shared our stories, prayed and wept, a wave of comfort came over me.

Losing someone you love is one the hardest things you will have to face. But face it we must. God, close friends and family will help us to make it through the storm. In the end, if we let him, God will perform his miracle and heal us of our pain.

4
A Biblical Perspective

When the perishable has been clothed with the imperishable, and the mortal with immortality, then the saying that is written will come true: "Death has been swallowed up in victory."

1 Corinthians 15:54

The heart of the wise is in the house of mourning.

Ecclesiastes 7:4

If we live, we live to the Lord; and if we die, we die to the Lord. So, whether we live or die, we belong to the Lord.

Romans 14:8

A fter defining the grief, loss and mourning process, I want to direct us to God's word and to his view of death and dying. Certainly this subject could be a book in itself. Therefore, this will not by any means be an exhaustive discussion. It is easy to lose sight of the Scriptures in our "feelings oriented" society. The following thoughts are for us to consider and are meant to be a springboard for deeper personal study. We will all be encouraged throughout this book to dig deeper into our Bibles, and any of the topics in this chapter would certainly be a good starting place. If we are prepared for the finish line, as Jesus and Paul were, we will run the race with the determination, confidence and faith needed to finish strong.

Loss Is Real

In John chapter 11 Jesus returns to Bethany where his friend Lazarus had died. When Jesus arrived at the home of Mary and Martha, he "was deeply moved in spirit and troubled," and upon approaching the tomb, he wept (John 11:33, 35, 38). These verses, among many, communicate to us that loss is real and that it is a painful and challenging experience. Loss is real because in death, the person is gone from us. This is the reality we are confronted with when a loved one dies.

Grief is common to both the Old Testament and the New Testament. We may tend to mitigate the grief of loss and death because of the New Testament promises of eternity and resurrection. In other words, we might think we should not feel loss so acutely anymore because we have the hope of resurrection. This is true but the Bible also teaches that loss is real and painful. We need to remember that Jesus felt the loss and was grieved by the death of his friend Lazarus despite the fact that he knew he would soon raise him from the dead (John 11:1–44). Loss is real and must be responded to appropriately, even in the face of resurrection and eternity.

Hopefully as a result of reading this book, you will learn some appropriate ways of responding to loss, grief and mourning. If you are bereaved or living with a terminal illness, be comforted by knowing that what you are going through is real and normal, and that Jesus went through emotional and physical suffering himself and wants to help you make it through as well.

The Example of Jesus

> But Christ has indeed been raised from the dead, the first-fruits of those who have fallen asleep. (1 Corinthians 15:20)

Our hope and example of what to expect in death is Jesus. The Bible tells us that he lived, died, was buried and was resurrected. Our hope is that the same process will happen with us as Christians. Jesus is called "the firstfruits" because he is the "earliest result of an endeavor," which is specifically God's resurrection work. Our soul will rejoin our new body, and we will be complete, ready to live in eternity with God. He has not given us all the details about the resurrection, heaven and eternity, but he has given us enough to have a conviction that the plan is in place. This should encourage us because this means that God has already planned the transition and wants us to feel secure about it. Furthermore, he has given us this picture of the finish line—or should we say the starting line—so that we will prepare now and run with purpose, determination and courage to the end. Death is not the end, but more accurately, the beginning of the beginning.

Jars of Clay

In 2 Corinthians 4–5 the apostle Paul painted a picture for us about life and death. He told us that our bodies are only "jars of clay" (4:7), mere breakable pottery, reminding us of the temporary nature of the physical body that we inhabit. He went on to share about the suffering that results from being a jar of clay. But then he offered an encouraging perspective:

> We do not lose heart. Though outwardly we are wasting away, yet inwardly we are being renewed day by day. For our light and momentary troubles are achieving for us an eternal glory that far outweighs them all. So we fix our eyes not on what is seen, but on what is unseen. For what is seen is temporary, but what is unseen is eternal. (2 Corinthians 5:16–18)

Our jar of clay, which is on the decline, houses the more significant part of us, the spiritual part, which is unseen and is constantly being renewed. A Christian's permanent body is the eternal one prepared for him. Paul called it "our heavenly dwelling" or our "imperishable...immortal" body into which we will be changed at the return of Jesus (2 Corinthians 5:2, 1 Corinthians 15:42). In the end the spiritual part of us (our soul) will be joined to our permanent eternal body. Our jar of clay will be changed into the new body "in the twinkling of an eye" (1 Corinthians 15:52), and we will continue our relationship with God on into eternity. This is our ultimate destiny and that which has always been planned for us by God himself.

Why did the Holy Spirit, through Paul, tell us all this? Probably because he knows that this perspective can be very contrary to our thinking. Both society and technology tell us just the opposite—that we are made to live a full, happy, long, non-suffering, "permanent" life here and now, not later. Instead, as Christians, we should be focused on real life, which is eternity, not what is temporary and seen. By faith, this must be how we think.

However, a focus on the eternal does not diminish, but rather confirms, the reality that we will suffer and have challenges in this life and with our jars of clay. But when we understand the bigger picture, we can have a real hope for the permanent life and body that God has prepared for us.

Pain and Suffering

A clay jar will deteriorate, crack, fade and eventually break. It will serve many purposes, but will never be indestructible. Our own jars of clay are very much the same. They deteriorate and are susceptible to war, climate, disease and the ill effects of man-made products. They have a certain life-span; they malfunction and can stop without warning. They are incredible machines and we do amazing feats with them, but they were never meant to be permanent. They were planned by God to be temporary housing of the more important part, the soul. The Bible has always been clear that whether by disaster, disease, an act of man or natural causes, all men will eventually physically die (see Ecclesiastes 3:1–8).

From the time of birth until the time of death, man will suffer in many different ways. It is a product of our nature and design. Though no one would solicit suffering, most of us will experience it at some point in our lifetime—and some for extended periods of time. Why is suffering such a big issue for us? It is because of the little question "Why?" Pain and suffering seem many times to be meaningless and unbearable. If you are the one in the middle of it, there is nothing comparable to it. When it reaches a certain threshold, the "Why?" question inevitably emerges: "Why did my mother suffer so much?" or "Why did God let my son die that way?" or "Why do I have cancer?" or "Why was my friend shot and killed?"

However, in the middle of pain and suffering, we must constantly seek to understand our existence from the Bible's perspective, or we will struggle with life's questions and possibly lose our faith and our eternal life as a result. It is important to approach the discussion of suffering in a Biblical way because we live in a time when society and technology would have us believe that pain and suffering are unwelcome, unjust and should be eliminated at all costs. This mind-set is contradictory to the Bible's acceptance of suffering as part—and even a purposeful part—of life (Romans 5:3–5, Hebrews 5:8, 1 Peter 4:1). Modern thinking tries to convince us medically, legally, benevolently and otherwise, that we have the power or are developing the power to alleviate and eliminate suffering. It insists that suffering should not exist. Yet if man says that suffering should not exist when in fact it does, he calls God and his love, power, goodness and will into question. The eventual outcome of such a position has man sitting in judgment of God.

None of this is meant to belittle the tremendous gains made in medicine and pain management. It is intended to remind us that in God's mind, pain and suffering are not the central issues in this life, but knowing him and preparing for eternal life are. It is the soul that is at the heart of God's design and work. He housed it in a jar of clay that is susceptible to war, pollution, disease, accident, famine and murder. The physical man can and will suffer and in the end, will die; but through faith and hope, the spiritual man will be raised and will receive a permanent body for eternity. This is the type of thinking that we need to embrace and live by because it is how God himself views life and death.

Let us not forget that God understands our pain and suffering. He has watched from the beginning of time what people have gone through and how they have mistreated others. He has witnessed thousands upon thousands of deaths due to war, disease, sickness and natural causes. He has listened to the cries of those in pain and who have suffered in all kinds of ways. He understands our pain and suffering and feels our pain and suffering, even firsthand. His experience of sending his own son to die a horrible and painful death for us tells us how much he understands us and cares for us. Needless to say, God draws near to us in our pain and helps us to face it, endure it and eventually overcome it.

The Double-Edged Sword

There is another side to the discussion of pain and suffering. Just as the sword described in Hebrews 4 has more than one purpose, so does pain and suffering. Suffering can cut and harm, but it also has the potential to cure and change. With pain there can be growth. Pain, while emotionally and physically trying, produces resilience, courage, endurance and determination. It calls for something greater from us and often gets it. Along with the devastation of death and dying comes transformation. Even though suffering has left many a person scarred and different, many have gone on to live and become something new and different. My favorite athlete, Lance Armstrong, cancer survivor and five-time winner of the Tour de France, is an example of those who learn that they were made "for a long, hard climb."[1] Others facing the pain exhort their fellow travelers to "dance":

> Promise me that you'll give faith a fighting chance,
> And when you get the choice to sit it out or dance,
> I hope you dance![2]

Whatever the situation, the ongoing narrative of life is filled with happiness and pain, joy and sorrow, life and death. We have the choice of how we will see and respond to this double-edged sword.

God's Will

Many times in the course of someone dying or at a time of death, onlookers will comment that it must be "God's will." In the face of suffering or death, God's will and power are often commented upon or called into question. Volumes have been written about these topics—clearly this brief section will raise questions for our further study and consideration. The following thoughts will hopefully provoke us to a deeper study of God's will.

A Spiritual Perspective

Simply put, we can look at death and dying from God's perspective or from ours. We will probably be tempted to play God by thinking, "If I were God, I would never have let the child die." However, this puts our finite, human judgments and interpretations above God's. We can only see circumstances from where we currently are in life, while God is outside of time, looking at the eternal picture. This kind of thinking is also dangerous because it can lead us to trust more in our feelings than in what we know and believe to be true. Granted, the circumstances surrounding dying and death bring intense emotional challenges and can send us into a mode of reevaluation, but we must decide to let God be God as we approach these challenging questions.

Know God

Our knowledge of God, as revealed in the Bible and in his creation, is a combination of mystery and revelation. There are things about God that will always remain a mystery. Look at the following scriptures:

> It is the glory of God to conceal a matter;
>   to search out a matter is the glory of kings.
> (Proverbs 25:2)

> The secret things belong to the LORD our God, but the things revealed belong to us and to our children forever, that we may follow all the words of this law. (Deuteronomy 29:29)

As you do not know the path of the wind,
    or how the body is formed in a mother's womb,
so you cannot understand the work of God,
    the Maker of all things. (Ecclesiastes 11:5)

"Truly you are a God who hides himself,
    O God and Savior of Israel." (Isaiah 45:15)

"For my thoughts are not your thoughts,
    neither are your ways my ways,"
declares the LORD.
"As the heavens are higher than the earth,
        so are my ways higher than your ways
        and my thoughts than your thoughts." (Isaiah
55:8–9)

Oh, the depth of the riches of the wisdom and knowledge
of God!
    How unsearchable his judgments,
    and his paths beyond tracing out! (Romans 11:33)

"For who has known the mind of the Lord
that he may instruct him?"
But we have the mind of Christ. (1 Corinthians 2:16)

These verses reveal that there is a depth to God that is beyond our human comprehension and will always remain a mystery. Having a spiritual perspective of God's will begins with recognizing this and respecting it. There may be some questions that are never answered this side of heaven, such as "Why did the child die?" There may be some answers we never receive here, such as "Why was the honorable, righteous, dedicated, young prophet John the Baptist beheaded at the whim of an angry woman?" A spiritual perspective leads a person to say, "There is more to this picture than I may understand, and it may remain beyond my comprehension, but I can live with that." To the worldly mind, and even to the Christian in the throes of grief and mourning, this may seem illogical, but to the spiritual mind, there is a realization that the logic of God is sometimes beyond our comprehension.

On the other hand, there are things that we *do know* about God's will because he has revealed them to us.

Natural laws. We know that God has created the world with laws that hold it together and cause it to function. Natural laws also are the reason that numerous deaths occur each year due to floods, hurricanes, earthquakes and the like. Also included in this category is the way we were physically designed, thus explaining why our bodies break down over time and may experience death by heart attack, stroke or old age.

Freedom of choice. We know from the Bible that God created man and gave him the ability to think, reason and create. We know that he gave him the freedom to choose and make decisions regarding his life. He also gave him the freedom to explore, not just in a physical way but in a spiritual way as well. Our prime example of this is Job, whom God allowed to raise questions, argue and wrestle openly with situations that happened to him. Moreover, freedom is the reason for many deaths that occur every year as a result of violence, suicide or accidents. It is also a contributor to deaths from diseases such as cancer because of pollution, toxins, poisons and other materials man has manufactured or created. We may wish none of these evils were around, but we must realize that to have them removed would entail the abandonment of human freedom and choice—including your own.

Purpose and mission. God has also revealed to man his purpose through his word: "Now it is God who has made us for this very purpose [to be clothed with our heavenly dwelling] and has given us the Spirit as a deposit, guaranteeing what is to come" (2 Corinthians 5:4–5). He has also revealed his mission for us through Jesus in Matthew 28:18–20:

> "Therefore go and make disciples of all nations, baptizing them in the name of the Father and of the Son and of the Holy Spirit, and teaching them to obey everything I have commanded you. And surely I am with you always, to the very end of the age."

God is clear that he desires for as many to be with him in heaven as possible (1 Timothy 2:3), and to that end he works in the world. He intervenes where he wills to guide situations so that people can have the opportunity to find him.

Those of us who are already Christians also know that God is committed to our circumstances also:

> And we know that in all things God works for the good of those who love him, who have been called according to his purpose. For those God foreknew he also predestined to be conformed to the likeness of his Son, that he might be the firstborn among many brothers. And those he predestined, he also called; those he called, he also justified; those he justified, he also glorified. What, then, shall we say in response to this? If God is for us, who can be against us? (Romans 8:28–31)

Thus we know that his will is to see that our outcome is a good one—and the eternal one implied here. He also gives Christians the help required to endure the challenges and difficulties along the way.

Plans. We know that God's ultimate will is carried out by his step-by-step plans. For example, to prevent and fight suffering in various forms, his plans include man seeing the need and doing his part with his fellow man. And his plans to comfort us in emotional pain and suffering also include man understanding and doing his part (see 2 Corinthians 1:3–7).

To summarize, knowing God involves understanding what is revealed about him and accepting that some things are beyond our comprehension. The will of God is like a vast ocean; we may swim on the surface or even dive to great depths, but we will never reach the bottom. However, he has revealed to us many things that help us understand our circumstances better, and he has given us the ability to endure the challenges that come. Most of all, he has committed himself to work the ultimate good for those who follow him.

'Was' vs. 'Within'

Many times we will hear it said, "*Was* it God's will that an innocent little boy was shot and killed?" This is a difficult question to answer, especially if you are one who believes that everything that occurs is somehow God's will. People who refuse to believe that sickness or death could be God's will leave themselves open to the possibility that he might not be as powerful as he says he is. Such is the dilemma. I prefer however, to view it somewhat differently. Is it God's will that a child should suffer and die? I say no. From the beginning, God has loved his creation and has favored life over death. In Genesis 3 God wanted Adam and Eve to enjoy life. He gave them a beautiful environment to live in and specifically warned them of the one situation that could destroy it. In Genesis 4, God urged Cain not to follow a path that would eventually take away life (his brother's) but to change and appreciate life. In both cases, God was for *life*, not death.

However, death is *within* God's will. *Was* the death of the innocent little boy who was shot and killed (like Abel, Cain's brother) God's will? No, but was it *within* the will of God? Yes. God does not will a child to suffer and die, but it is within his will. As we saw above, in God's revealed will, he gives man freedom, and man in turn can choose how to use it—by promoting life or by using it to destroy others, such as when a man shoots and kills an innocent child. God's desire is for life, but death occurs within his will in the ways we learned about above, such as through natural laws and human freedom. It is important for us to understand this, and then communicate it in a right way, whenever and wherever appropriate.

Time May Make It Clear

We need to give God's will time. He gives us the freedom to explore circumstances, to ask questions, to search for answers and meaning, and to present our arguments to him. In time we may learn to see things differently. We may discover Bible truths that we did not know existed or had never quite understood. We just need to remember to respect the fact that he is infinite and beyond our comprehension. We may not find all answers regarding his will, but in time, we may come to understand more and more.

Life Is Eternal

We must never lose sight of the fact that God's will has secured life, eternal life, for us. This is reality, as well as the best deal going! It is part of the revealed will of God that is found in his word (John 3:16). It is the reality that should help us to accept the fact that God's will often is beyond our comprehension, and enable us to endure the challenges that are found in a world of living and dying.

Hopefully this challenges your thinking regarding God's will and gives you some direction for further Bible study. Someone once commented that he would not want to follow a "God" that he could completely figure out or explain. God's will guarantees this, but it also reveals much about the tremendously loving God whom we serve. I am convinced that God wants us to have a clearer picture of his will so that we will not be too quick to blame him for something he does not do—or to walk away from him because we cannot understand. But in the end, he has revealed more than enough about his heart and motives to allow us to confidently place our trust in him.

Faith Is the Victory

> ...everyone born of God overcomes the world. This is the victory that has overcome the world, even our faith.
> (1 John 5:4)

The victory in this life will be our faith. We will not find all the answers. We will not solve all the mysteries. When all is said and done, our faith will be what carries us through. Whether we are in the midst of enormous pain and suffering or we are helping those who are, we will need faith to overcome this world. Let us continue to believe in the God who loves and cares for us. Let us continue to believe and trust in his eternal plan for us. Let us continue to believe that his word is useful for equipping us for life and death. And in the end, by God's power, we will overcome this world and all its struggles by our faith and sing that old song, "This World Is Not My Home":

O Lord, you know I have no friend like you,
If heaven's not my home then Lord what will I do?
The angels beckon me from heaven's open door,
And I can't feel at home in this world anymore.

In Summary

I want to encourage you to continue to study and meditate on the following areas:

- The example of Jesus in dealing with death
- The inevitability of suffering and death
- A spiritual view of the will of God
- The need for a maturing faith to face the challenges of suffering and death

This chapter is not an attempt to provide exact answers to the serious and complex issues surrounding death and dying, but rather, to urge you to begin a deeper investigation of them on your own. Each of us must have our own convictions and faith to walk the road that lies ahead, to go on our mourning journeys.

When my husband died, keeping a daily journal was one of the most helpful things for me. It was certainly difficult to write out my feelings, fears and thoughts. It made them more starkly real, but on the other hand, it helped me deal with them honestly. It kept me from stuffing and going on—only to have to deal with stuffed feelings years later.

—Melanie

5
To the Bereaved

A good friend of mine lost a number of family members in the last two years. With each additional death we wondered if he would survive. If you knew Frank like I do, you would notice that his characteristic smile is missing and that at times he seems to be in a daze, not connecting with what is happening around him. Shortly after his most recent loss, Frank told me he simply wanted to withdraw and do nothing. At times he would cry incessantly and would noticeably turn inward, closing out the world around him at a moment's notice. He began to erratically attend what used to be significant activities in his life, and when he did show up, he left hurriedly and without explanation. Attempts to reach out to him were met with stiff resistance. When his wife tried to force him to get help, Frank got angry and irritated. He seemed to sink deeper and deeper into a hole that no one could help him out of.

In the middle of these dark moments, however, he began to do certain small things. He started to read books that addressed his particular issues of loss. He would ask questions about death and about his own reactions to it. He attended a reunion commemorating the first anniversary of the death of his mother and listened as others shared stories and memories of her life. Listening to others talk about their loss helped him and motivated him, in turn, to share his own story.

Frank made trips home, and while there he gathered mementos that reminded him of the members of his family who had died. He kept many of these, but others he gave away to people who he felt could use them or would come to know his deceased family member better by receiving something that represented the kind of person she was. As much as he wanted at times to "go off and die," he forced himself to once more begin attending the activities he had previously been devoted to. Even though his emotions would often rage, he was determined not to hide them and openly displayed them, even in group settings. At one point he considered joining a bereavement group; but by the time he found one, he felt things were improving and decided to wait, at least for now.

Today Frank will tell you things are getting better. He is different, but is engaged again with life around him. He continues to find ways to deal with his losses that are teaching him how to live without people he loved. He is at this point only because he decided to take the steps that he could take—no more, no less. On the very day that I wrote these words, something happened that has given me reason to believe Frank will be all right: for the first time in months, he told me a joke.

To Help Your Hurt

I often receive calls from people who are grieving. It is hard to describe the pain and emotions that flood my phone and living room at these times, and yet there are some common denominators. I have found without exception that the bereaved need someone to tell them that they are okay, that what they are going through is normal. They want someone to sit with them and let them have their pain—without fixing it for them. They want people to know that mourning does not end in a few months or even years, but may last a lifetime. They want others to know that they are the ones who have to walk through this journey and that they must do it as *their* faith allows them to, not as others' faith would.

If you are bereaved, this chapter is for you. I hope you have been helped in ways that comforted, encouraged and sustained you in your most difficult days. I would like to suggest that there are many resources available to you, such as books, Internet sites and support groups. Some of these are mentioned at the end of this book. The following thoughts are intended to provide some simple yet specific help for you at this difficult time. I have purposefully kept the list short, however, knowing that you have a lot to think through and deal with already. (At the end of this chapter I have also included a few additional spiritual notes for you to consider.)

Yield to Grief

In the wake of the death of Lazarus, "Jesus wept" (John 11:35). As we have discussed in earlier chapters, you must deal with your grief at some time. It cannot be put off indefinitely. You may be tempted to think that if you allow yourself to grieve, you will not be able to stop or control it. But take heart—you can face it and get through it. It is possible to work through the emotions and life changes following a death and not be destroyed by the experience. This may be exactly opposite of the way you feel at the moment, but with God's help you can do it. Make a decision to allow yourself to grieve.

One thing that may help you to get started is making time to grieve. Determine a period of time that you will grieve. For instance, set aside from 1:00 to 3:00 PM as a time that you will spend grieving, after which you will get up and continue with daily activities. During this time you can reflect on the relationship, look at photo albums, visit the grave (if possible) or share stories with someone else about your loved one. Use the time for whatever helps connect you with the person in a meaningful way and subsequently helps you get in touch with your feelings for her.

Also, a word of caution is in order here, given the fact that not all relationships were good ones. Difficult relationships can bring a mixture of responses that must be acknowledged and addressed in some way. I would encourage you to yield to grief in this instance as well. To prolong the decision to acknowledge a relationship, good or bad, can only cause problems in coming to terms with the relationship and in eventually incorporating the loss into your life.

For those of you who feel that all you do is grieve, you should do the opposite with time. Set aside a time that you will not grieve and will do other activities such as exercise, chores or reading. This can keep you from constantly being overwhelmed. Be patient during this process. Give yourself time and do not let yourself feel rushed by others' perceptions of how long grief should last and how you should handle it.

Expect Other Issues to Come Up

Don't be surprised if grief brings up other losses or other challenging issues from your past, such as abuse, forgiveness, traumatic episodes and family issues. Losses tend to resurrect the pain of prior losses. It may be that you will need to revisit a prior death and work through any areas of distress or difficulty that are still unresolved. Also you may find that because of the death, you now feel vulnerable in other areas of your life. A death may unleash your fears about prior challenging situations, expose immature areas in your character and reveal things in your life that you might have thought were settled, but really were not. If such "unfinished business" should arise, consider getting appropriate help for the specific challenge that you are dealing with. Often these issues require resolution before you can work through your present grief.

Reexamining your relationship with the deceased is one of the hurdles you will face when mourning. Coming to grips with the kind of person the deceased really was—warts and all—can be tough, especially when the relationship was close. Issues that surface as you proceed will need to be addressed and dealt with, including issues of omission as well as commission (things she did not do as well as things she did do). Some examples are unresolved arguments, unfair financial dealings and abuse. These issues can be difficult to raise if you were the one "sinned against" by the deceased. Spiritual concerns such as, "I never told her _____" or "I wish I had shared with her about my relationship with God" will need to be confronted as well. Failing to acknowledge such regrets and get help dealing with them can cause you to harden your heart and grow bitter and resentful.

Be prepared—relationship challenges may abound within a family after a death. Some of the worst dynamics can be struggles for power and possessions, disputes over arrangements, and bad attitudes about everything in between. Grief can become complicated by arguments, difficult decisions and hurt feelings regarding family issues. Do not be caught off guard by these happenings. Even though your heart may be severely tested in many ways, refuse to fall back into unhealthy patterns you may have had in dealing with your family in the past. You need to remain righteous in the way you treat them. It can help to have someone outside the family assist you in sorting out your feelings and in determining your participation in resolving any family disputes.

On the positive side, families can grow in strength and unity during times of crisis and stress. You may even see family members change for the better as they observe your example and the way you conduct yourself in handling the family dynamics.

Take Care of Yourself

Grief is hard on you physically as well as emotionally. Do the best you can to exercise, get rest and eat properly. You only increase the degree of difficulty of grieving when you allow your health, order or routine to deteriorate. If you feel like the difficulty is increasing and physically or mentally things are getting worse, then you might need to see your doctor. You may need medication or other therapies to help you get back on track. Also, if you find it challenging to sit through a church service or similar activity without crying (because the activity is something you and the deceased did together), feel free to get up and take a walk. Don't feel you need to be an example of great self-control by sitting there in distress at a moment when you need to be grieving. If you have to cry, then cry. If you need to express your emotions, then do so.

Also, it is good at times to take a "day off" from grieving. To do so does not make a statement about your lack of love for the person who died—it simply gives you some time to think, regain some energy, do some chores and provide the mental relief that is much needed for mourning. God is well aware of your need to stay healthy and take care of yourself, and he will provide you with the opportunity to do so: "He makes me to lie down in green pastures, he leads me beside quiet waters, he restores my soul" (Psalm 23:2–3). Let God help you take care of yourself.

Stay in Touch with Friends

Try not to isolate yourself. Proverbs 17:17 says, "A friend loves at all times, and a brother is born for adversity." Stay close to people. It can be tempting to close the door emotionally and protect yourself when people do not understand your grief and say or do the wrong things. However, in the end, your relationships—even though not always perfect—will help you through the long, challenging time of mourning. Instead of pulling away, seek help from friends or from others who understand bereavement. They can give you perspective and support when others fail to provide it.

Be Your Own Advocate

While friends tried to comfort Job in his mourning, at one point he felt it necessary to declare, "You are worthless physicians, all of you! If only you would be altogether silent! For you, that would be wisdom" (Job 13:4–5). As challenging as it may seem, there will be times when you will need to teach others about your grief. Do it! Sometimes this is the only way they will learn about grief and mourning and how to respond better to the needs of the bereaved and their families. Because you are the one going through it, you may need to be the teacher on many occasions. Be kind, be gentle, but be honest.

In the end you will help not only yourself but others as well.

Also, there may be times when you are left to accomplish certain tasks on your own, such as finding out specific information related to the death, settling family matters, dealing with insurance companies or hospitals and resolving estate issues. Whatever situation arises, handle it the best you can. Whenever possible, get help and advice from others regarding legal, financial, medical issues and other topics. We are not always clear minded when making these important decisions, and an objective outsider can help. Ask for this advice from qualified people or from someone experienced enough to lend spiritual as well as practical wisdom to your decisions. People are often ready to help, but may not know the magnitude of the help you need unless you inform them. Make sure that you have someone to talk to in order to avoid any misunderstandings about your expectations for receiving help and to have a forum for working through any attitudes that might arise in the event that something is not getting done.

Last, a day may come when you are asked to share publicly about your experience with death. You should do this only when you are ready. Since many of us have a misinformed view of the length of the mourning process, people can ask for your participation way too soon after your loss. You should not feel obligated to speak publicly because someone has asked. Be honest, straightforward and share with them why, when or where you would like to or not like to speak about it. This way, you will not do a disservice to your own feelings and will keep others better informed of where you are in your mourning process.

Find an Advocate

Just as you must be your own advocate during grief and mourning, at times you will need an outside advocate, someone to speak up for you. Just as Jesus promises to be our spiritual advocate (1 John 2:1), we all need others to help us in difficult situations. An advocate can listen, explain to others how you are doing, find specific help for your particular challenges, mediate difficult relationships, and more. He or she can help you sort through your thoughts, give you perspective, and help you deal with others' responses to you. Look for someone who will listen and be there with you for the long haul.

Accept Help

The wise writer of Ecclesiastes wrote, "If one falls down, his friend can help him up" (Ecclesiastes 4:10). Let people help you. This is what family and friends are for. Be specific about the real help (prayers, cards, chores, meals, etc.) you need. If you are not up to determining what help you need, give someone else permission to create a list for you and find the appropriate people to complete it.

Help Yourself

The Apostle Paul was a great example of someone who constantly shared what was going on in his life, even his intense emotions (see 2 Corinthians 1:8–11). I believe he did this not only because he was honest, but also because he knew that it helped him work through things. When dealing with death, you can help yourself by expressing your feelings and emotions. It can be damaging mentally and physically to hold things in. You may be tempted to "stuff" your emotions because you think that others will not be able to handle them or that you may get out of control or that you will be undignified. Grief is grief. God designed us with emotions and knows they come out when we are grieving. Allow yourself to express your emotions and feelings truthfully (see Ephesians 4:25, Colossians 3:9, 2 Corinthians 4:2). If some "rules" for expression would make you feel better at this point, then the following may help: (1) you are not allowed to hurt yourself; (2) you are not allowed to hurt others; and (3) you are not allowed to hurt any property.

Grief does not give us the right to mistreat people nor the license to vent our frustrations about life at the expense of others. You can learn to express your emotions in a healthy way, and others around you can learn to accept them and work with you to handle them. Talking is very helpful in this regard. Find understanding people with whom you can talk and tell them what is going on inside. Talking can release the anger, sadness, fear and other feelings that settle in the heart. Talking to others helps you to sound out your thinking about yourself, decisions you need to make and possibly other issues that have come up after the death that require help or resolution. And talking can keep you from becoming isolated.

In addition, reading can be helpful. Books such as Earl Grollman's *Living When a Loved One Has Died* touch on the initial issues and responses to death.[1] Writers like Therese Rando *(How to Go on Living When Someone You Love Dies)* cover grief and mourning in a very thorough way and give sound instruction and help with death and loss.[2] Reading helps to give you a clearer picture of your situation. The better you understand grief and mourning, the better you can help yourself.

On a related note, writing may help you. Recording thoughts and feelings in a journal can be an effective way of getting things out so that you can deal with them more specifically.

Last, helping others can be a way of helping yourself. The action of giving allows you to get outside yourself (Philippians 2:1–4). It diverts your attention from yourself and your grief and reconnects you with others and with the world around you. It presents you with the opportunity to help someone else and at the same time, restores some needed joy in your heart as you do so.

Keep a Bond

It is okay to keep a connection to your loved one. The Bible shows us that the Jews continued to keep alive the memory of their great spiritual leaders from generation to generation (Exodus 3:15). After a death we naturally seek to keep the connection to the deceased alive in our hearts. This is generally true of all deaths except when the relationship was a negative experience and a continuing connection is not wanted. It is especially true when a child dies. Parents do not want to forget or lose their child, nor do they want to give up the relationship and say good-bye. You will need to be the one to determine how to carry forward the relationship with the deceased. You may create your own ritual that helps you remember the deceased in a good and healthy way, maybe in some special activity at a particular time of the year. You may want to keep certain objects that remind you of her (1 Samuel 7:12). Some people create videos or memory books about their loved one. Also, there are support groups (such as Compassionate Friends) and books available to you (see the resources in the back of this book) that can help you with this issue. Whatever you choose to do, remember that you do not need to feel that you are leaving the person behind as you move ahead with life. You can still keep alive the memories and remembrances of her in your heart as you continue on without her.

Make Sense of the Loss

At some point you will look for meaning in the death. This may be elusive for some and simple for others (see chapters 3 and 4 for some spiritual thoughts to consider). One way to help with this search is to keep a journal of your experiences. Author C. S. Lewis wrote a journal after the death of his wife called *A Grief Observed* in which he moves through many thoughts, feelings and questions about God and the spiritual side of death. By writing, he forced himself to think through the meaning of his wife's death and his response to it. This is not to say everyone has to write, but it provides one way of sorting out your thinking. Also, if you are looking for spiritual help, it is very important to bring your questions and thoughts to God. He wants to hear from you, and he wants you to dig down into his word to get help with your thinking. You may need to go back and study through scriptures that comfort you or challenge your faith. In either case this study will help you to rethink what God has to say about life and death, and if you continue on, it will present you with a chance to find meaning in your loss. Other people can listen and help as well. Remember that your church family should be the place to get the help, love, support and truth that you need as you search for meaning in the loss of your loved one.

Special Bereavement Situations

Complicated Bereavement

Complicated deaths can bring about complicated bereavement. For instance, a suicide presents us with a host of questions that other deaths do not, such as "What was wrong with me that they had to do this?" or "What could I have done to prevent this?" It also has challenges that are not associated with a typical death, like a police investigation and other legal complications. These can in turn bring about spiritual complications such as greater guilt, issues of forgiveness, the social stigmatization of suicide and questions regarding the destiny of the deceased. This struggle is heightened especially if the deceased had physical or mental challenges (such as depression or low self-esteem). Therefore, in the event of a suicide, or another complicated death, there are specific challenges that can make mourning more difficult spiritually. If you are in one of these mourning situations, how should you face the challenges?

Obtain Information

You should be active in obtaining information. Sometimes Christians are not aggressive in finding out information about a complicated death such as a car accident. But Jesus used the example of the widow to teach about persistence (Luke 18:1–8). It is okay for a Christian to be persistent about obtaining legal documents, medical reports, police reports, insurance benefits and more. These are often vital in helping you piece together facts that are important for you to know. Many times when people have received more information and have understood the circumstances surrounding the death more clearly, it has enabled them to continue along in the mourning process and not remain "stuck."

Be Patient with Yourself

Complicated deaths may take longer to work through than others. Your mourning may be interrupted by events connected to the death, such as a murder that takes years to come to trial. You will have to be patient with yourself and not have the burdening expectation that says you have to be finished with mourning in a "timely fashion." God will help you to find a way to deal with it if you continue to trust him and look to him for strength.

Seek Help

If you feel that dysfunction seems to be growing in your mourning, you should not hesitate to seek spiritual and professional help. Talk to spiritual people who are mature and have experience in dealing with your situation. If this type of support is lacking or not helping you, then don't be afraid to seek professional help.

Suicide

If you are a suicide survivor, consider the following:

- If the suicide is recent, have you received any specific help from suicide support groups or counselors? If you have not, then I encourage you to seek out such support as soon as possible. There are many issues that come up after a suicide that warrant getting input on what survivors normally go through. Generally the sooner you get support, the better, and most often the best help comes from another survivor.

- Get information. If you are hesitant to reach out for support, contact the number in the resource section of this book and ask to be sent information on surviving suicide. Reading may encourage you to open up to other means of help.

- If you are wrestling with spiritual questions regarding a suicide, then find someone you can confide in who will respect your confidentiality. Putting this off will only cause your faith to falter at some point.

- If you lived through a suicide some time ago, you may need to ask yourself the following questions: (1) How am I doing? (2) Do I have any unresolved issues related to the death? (3) Are there questions that I never asked that still bother me? (4) Has it changed my perspective on life and God in a negative way? It is never too late to deal with these issues. It may be that you never really grieved the loss due to the fact that you were confused about how to do so. Given that our society often hides suicide, you may have responded in the same way and subsequently did not mourn the death the way you needed to. You may need to talk with someone who understands this type of death and let them help you determine if there are issues that need some discussion and resolution.

Spiritual Notes

Stay Close to God

You will keep hope alive if you stay close to God. As much as you are able, continue to read and pray. Do not stop talking and listening to God. For example, here is the "weeping prophet," Jeremiah, expressing his heart about the suffering and death of the people as Jerusalem was destroyed:

> I remember my affliction and my wandering,
>   the bitterness and the gall.
> I well remember them,
>   and my soul is downcast within me.
> Yet this I call to mind
>   and therefore I have hope:
>
> Because of the Lord's great love we are not consumed,
>   for his compassions never fail.
> They are new every morning;
>   great is your faithfulness.
> I say to myself, "The Lord is my portion;
>   therefore I will wait for him." (Lamentations 3:19–24)

Reading the Psalms can bring you comfort and help. Even though you may not remember what you read at times, keep reading. The Holy Spirit will work through the Word to help you get through this and to keep you connected to God. Read passages just to let the words comfort and console you. Read and listen to the cries and pains of others, such as David in the Psalms, and know that you are not alone. Read as much as you can as often as you can. Remember to be patient with yourself in this whole process. Don't feel guilty if you are not having what you consider to be incredible, life-changing times with God. Grief can leave you numb, distracted, confused, unable to concentrate and emotionally drained to the point of not even wanting to spend time with the Lord. So, just do the best you can. God knows that in grief it is often the case that "the spirit is willing, but the body is weak" (Mark 14:38). And yet he loves you and is walking beside you all the way.

The following are some passages that offer hope and comfort.

Psalm 18:30–36	Isaiah 64:4
Psalm 23	Jeremiah 17:7–8
Psalm 34:17–19	Lamentations 3:19–26
Psalm 37:7–8	John 5:24
Psalm 139	2 Corinthians 1:3–4
Psalm 61	2 Corinthians 4:16–18
Psalm 69	Hebrews 13:5
Proverbs 24:16	Revelation 21:3–4
Isaiah 40:28–31	

Pray

Is anyone of you in trouble? He should pray. (James 5:13)

Pray! Let God know how you feel, how you are really doing. Lay it out. Let him know the truth. Do your best to be honest with God. When David was in trouble he put it all out on the table. (See Psalms 10, 22 and 74 for examples.) When you experience difficult deaths you need to pray. There will not be tidy answers to tough situations like SIDS. You will need to pray that God will get you through even if the answers do not come. Pray even if you are angry. The more that can't be explained, the more your anger may grow. You might feel that God is the reason for the lack of information as well as other things. Lay your anger out before God. He is listening and will not turn away even if you are angry. God can handle anything that you can throw at him, especially your anger and questions. Being honest with him will keep your heart soft and will keep issues out in the open that could potentially separate you from him. You may well look back on this time of anguish and heartfelt prayer as a model for identifying and expressing your emotions to God and for thinking and working through your relationship with him. Though your connection with God may be shaken by loss, do not let go of him. His word will reach and enlarge your heart, his ear will hear your pain, and his love will sustain you through grief and provide for your needs.

Be Patient with Spiritual Questions

In Luke 13, Jesus addressed the judgment of the general public regarding the death of some Galileans on whom a tower had fallen. He challenged the conclusion drawn by the crowd regarding the spirituality of the victims and then delivered a righteous judgment on the Galileans as well as on all who were present. One lesson to be learned from this, especially in dealing with death, is to be patient and not rush to judgment about spiritual issues like the crowd did. If you have spiritual questions, resist the urge to immediately answer and resolve everything. The onset of acute grief is not the time to sort everything out, and attempting to do so may frustrate you more than help you. You need to trust that God will provide the right time and place to review the spiritual issues surrounding the death, to search for meaning and to raise your questions. He alone knows exactly when you are ready to listen and work through things. And it is important to accept that some questions take a long time to answer.

On the other hand, you may be tempted to avoid this type of spiritual discussion altogether if your loved one was not a Christian. You need to deal with it, however. To ignore this issue for a long period of time will give Satan an opportunity to erode your faith and conviction about the truth and ultimately to attempt to destroy your relationship with God.

Confront the Complicated Issues

Complicated deaths may raise spiritual questions that require help to answer. Terrorist acts (like those of September 11), floods, school shootings, earthquakes and the like often raise questions about suffering and evil. Time, Bible study and help from others are required as you struggle with these difficult questions (see chapters 4 and 10). Sometimes, even after all this, there may not be a suitable answer for you. At these junctures you may need to make a decision to live with the fact that there is no clear answer. In time, after further pursuit and study, you may decide differently. However, confront the questions the best that you can. Do not allow Satan to work in your heart by generating negative feelings and bad attitudes about questions that do relate to your situation, such as "How could God allow someone to go into a school and kill innocent children?" Find someone you trust, and talk. Your mourning may depend on how well you open up and talk about the questions you are wrestling with in your heart and address them in a righteous way.

Don't Give Up on God

Deaths can bring up a lot of "Whys?" David asked "why" many times in his life. Job asked for answers repeatedly, but only received one, which was who God is. In complicated deaths there may never be a complete answer to the question "Why?" But I believe that Paul was trying to teach us about the things in life that we can hang on to when he says, "And now these three remain: faith, hope and love" (1 Corinthians 13:13). Faith says that you can still trust God when all reason fails, when there is no suitable answer or "it just doesn't make any sense." Faith says that I will not walk out on God, even though the pain at time seems unbearable. Next, you need to hang on to the hope that some day you will understand more than you do now—or at least that God will likely explain it to you when you see him face to face. Keep looking, searching and asking. Finally, love is right there as God surrounds you with it in your loss—love in the form of friends and family, love that would do anything for you in time of need, love that will help you carry your burden, and the love between you and God, which no complicated death—nor any other kind of death—can ever destroy.

If you are bereaved, I hope you found this chapter to be helpful and not overwhelming. These suggestions are offered with help in mind, yet knowing full well that you have the final say in how you will deal with your loss. I hope that you will, like my friend in the opening story, continue to take the necessary steps, however large or small, to learn to live again and to stay close to God.

My Story
The Loss of My Teenage Daughter
Carol Massengil

On August 28, 1979, Tracey Marie Massengill was born to Ron and me. What a sweet little thing she was with her black hair and dark eyes. We lived in Hartsville, Tennessee, at the time, along with our other two children, Charissa and Dusty. We were part of a small group of Christians who have sustained us through the years. We helped each other with births, weddings and, now, funerals. Tracey died on February 11, 1998. She was eighteen years old. She died of pneumonia after several ravaging months of a battle with anorexia.

Her doctors have said we will never know why Tracey became anorexic. We do know she fought it with an athlete's tenacity, and loved God with all her heart. So, Ron and I are left with all the after-effects of having a child die. I had sometimes wondered what I would do if my husband died. But, never did I entertain the thought that one of my children might die. That just doesn't happen. It's not supposed to happen. But it did. It happened suddenly and without warning. As Tracey lay in the hospital, people, literally all over the world, prayed and begged God for her life. And God was silent. Northside Hospital in Atlanta was absolutely bursting at the seams with our friends—so much so that the staff had to open another waiting room. How we are loved! Still, God was silent. Then, on Wednesday at 5:10 PM God spoke. He said, "No." And, that was it. No more negotiation, no more pleading. God had said no. And we were left to deal with it.

The first days and weeks were absolutely horrible. We felt as if we swam around in a huge pool of pain and came up periodically for breaths of air, and each breath was excruciating. I drank water incessantly, and I've since learned this is the body's response to crying huge pools of tears! One night I started crying and couldn't stop. Ron had to call a close friend to come over just to be with me; that helped so much. Each member of our family grieved differently. It was hard watching our other children mourn. They wanted and needed to feel her nearness and the closeness of friends.

The first thing I had to come to grips with was how God could say no to me when he knew how much I loved him, and how much Tracey loved him. He had always answered my prayers. But now, I couldn't even feel God anymore. It was two weeks before I could open my Bible, and, even then, I could only read the Psalms. After two weeks I began to go for walks in the sunshine again, and I tried to talk to God, but he wasn't talking back. I began to look for someone to blame. If I couldn't blame God, then I would just blame the doctor, or what about that boy who had hurt her in high school. But, no, that's not healthy to blame people; so the only person left to blame was myself. Believe me, I have spent many fruitless hours trying to figure out what I did wrong. After all, a mother's job is to protect her child, and I had failed.

For a few months I couldn't feel God at all, but I think he was watching carefully, letting me feel just a little more and a little more. I felt terrified of God. I felt anger like David did when Uzzah was struck dead for touching the ark. A friend told me to read the book *Trusting God* over and over and over until I believed it.[1] So I did...three times. It helped me feel God again. I realized that I cannot live without God.

About this time, I began to see how unlike God I am. God freely sacrificed his precious son so all the rest of us could go to heaven. I didn't want to sacrifice my child for anyone. I began to feel a kinship with Mary as she watched Jesus die before her eyes. She watched the blood flow down his body, and breathed with him each agonizing breath. I, too, watched my child suffer unbelievably as she died. It must have seemed so senseless to Mary, as it did to me. I felt Mary and I were one until I thought about the fact that two of her sons died a martyr's death. Truly, a sword pierced her soul. Mary suffered far more than I could ever begin to know. I cannot wait to meet that precious woman.

At first, the hardest part was coming to grips with what my own part was in Tracey's death. And there were my own sinful responses to situations. I felt jealous when I would see another family with three kids. Also, another family's daughter who was anorexic went into the hospital with a brain injury, and ended up being healed, and no longer anorexic as a result of the brain trauma. I thought, *God, why couldn't that have been Tracey?* What helped was those families didn't ignore what had happened. They talked about it and grieved with us. It's amazing what bringing things out in the open can do.

And, then there was the anger. Ron said there are no more restaurants in town I can go to because I've had a fight with all the managers. Ron and I are different in our grief. I may feel angered if someone calls to get help with their teenage daughter, while Ron is glad to help. I feel encouraged if someone says, "It will get better with time," while Ron isn't.

Something that must be hard for our friends is, *what in the world should I say to comfort these crazy people?* I don't have a lot of help for you there. We're in a club that you don't want to be in, believe me. One day it's okay to call and the next day it's not. The best thing to do is say I'm sorry, and leave it at that. It's human nature to want to fix grieving people, but try to refrain. Job's friends genuinely wanted to help him, but they should have left after the seven days of silence. At first people said to me, "People will become Christians because of Tracey's death." And, of course, that's true, and I believe they have. But, at the time, I didn't want anyone to become a Christian because of my child's death. I just wanted her back. It was too soon to hear that.

Our church here in Atlanta has been so good to Ron and me. And our families have loved us and comforted us in so many ways. I pushed my parents away for awhile. Don't ask me why. I think it was just too painful to face them without all my children. I felt humiliated. I don't know if they knew that, but they gave me the space I needed. They never pushed or prodded; they've just been there whenever I wanted them. We're close again.

Our children and their spouses comfort and strengthen us. Ron and I comfort each other in ways no one else can. We are each the only one who truly knows the loss that the other one feels. I am so grateful to have a husband who loves me. Our biggest comfort so far came on Christmas Day: a little 6 lb. 1 oz. baby boy, Spencer Reese Bright. Ron and I are absolutely eaten up with being grandparents. We decided that there is something magical about the bond between grandparents and their grandchildren: both think the other is perfect. Recently I told God, "You can start calling me Naomi now instead of Mara, because I am truly comforted."

Even in the happy things, there is always a huge hole. Rarely a day passes that Ron and I don't cry a little bit for our precious daughter. Sometimes I write her letters and ask God to read them to her. The thing that I can say about what has happened with the passage of time is, at first, the pain was torrential; then somewhere along the way we had an okay day. Now the truly bad days are only occasional. What we say is, sometimes we're happy, but we're never not sad. Each day takes on deep meaning for me. I ride a mountain bike, and I'm learning to play the violin. Ron and I love to ride his motorcycle around the Georgia mountains. These are spiritual things for me; I believe God wants us to feel him intensely, and to supremely enjoy the world he has created for us. And I do. But, like the first century Christians, I long with all of my soul for heaven. I'm ready to go anytime.

6
Helping the Bereaved

Mourn with those who mourn.

Romans 12:15

B ill is an older man who has a genuine care and concern for people no matter what their age, race, economic or educational status. You might say that the thing that stands out about Bill is that he is always there. While working in the same church together, we saw a large number of deaths in a short period of time. They ranged from the accidental death of a child to the old-age death from natural causes. At every wake and funeral there was Bill. Many times when I was speaking to a bereaved family member or friend I was amazed to hear that Bill had already been by to see them or had dropped off a card or food or had shoveled their driveway. Neither time nor the intensity of grief seemed to deter Bill. I have seen him at a wake with a distraught weeping friend just sitting there holding his hand and being with him. He has not had training in death education nor does he profess to know all the right things to say, but he shows up when there is a need and he does whatever he can to help. He does not fear the pain and grief that come with loss, but welcomes them as a fact of life that calls for compassion and companionship, for volunteers to walk with you through it.

Another thing about Bill is that he is still in there serving people long after the death. I find this quality one of the most amazing and inspiring things about him. It can be easy to help in the moment of need, but to follow up with a bereaved wife or teenage son long after the death is what defines Bill as someone who really helps people. For many it is a hard thing to stay in touch with the bereaved after a death. In fact the bereaved will tell you that most people don't. Bill, however, is the other side of the story. He does what he can to call, drop a card, run an errand or remember a special date. He is not fulfilling a church program or "volunteering"; he is just meeting a need. If you try to praise him for it, he will dismiss it by telling you, "It was only a phone call" or "It didn't take but a minute."

I feel connected to Bill not because of having spent a lot of time with him, but because of his commitment to comfort and console others. He encourages me and makes me feel secure in the knowledge that friends like him are ready to respond when I or anyone else needs them. However, I think the greatest testimony about Bill comes from those he has helped. Many will tell you outright how much they appreciate him and all he has done for them, but what I see is more of the unspoken communication and connection that he has with them. The strong, invisible ties of pain and death have bound them together, evidenced by the look in the eye, the hand on the arm and the closeness that speaks of deeper friendship.

Bill will always be one of the greatest heroes in life to me. He is moved by his relationship with God and his love for people to be a man who helps those who are in one of life's most challenging circumstances—bereavement.

Bill helps us begin this chapter by providing for us a great example of how to help the bereaved. In chapter 1 we defined a bereaved person as one who had suffered a loss. Be sure to read chapters 1 through 3 before reading this section so that you will have a better understanding of how to apply or think about the suggestions listed below. The following list is by no means exhaustive and is in fact limited so as not to over-whelm you with a long list of things that "must" be done.

Helping Early On

Pray and Stay Humble

Pray for wisdom as James 1:5 talks about. Pray for God to lead you in helping the bereaved. Pray to be able to sit and lis-ten to another person's pain, not trying to fix him or his situ-ation. Be humble. Be open to learning and not feeling as though you must provide all the answers. Allow your own view of God to be enlarged by the pain and suffering of oth-ers. Be humbled by the fact that you are privileged to serve the bereaved in one of the greatest hours of human need.

Consider the Person

Paul taught that we are to "look...to the interests of oth-ers" (Philippians 2:4). Try to understand what the loss means to the bereaved person and what he is going through. Consider these questions: Who was the deceased to him? What was their relationship like? How might the type of death affect him? Was he dealing with any challenging life issues prior to the death? What might be especially difficult for him with regard to this loss? When you take the time to consider bereaved people and their situations, you will be more aware of what they are dealing with and will be in a better position to help them. Keep in mind that you cannot remove their loss or pain nor fix their situation, but you can be there for them in a more understanding way as they walk through it. See chapter 3 for some additional insights on ministering in an individual way to the bereaved.

Reach Out

Luke tells us that one day Jesus saw the funeral procession of a young boy, the only son of a widow. When he saw her, "his heart went out to her." Then he "went up and touched the coffin" (Luke 7:13–15). Jesus did not let death back him away, and neither should you. Obviously, I am not encouraging the interrupting of funeral processions, but simply urging you to reach out to the bereaved. Your presence with those who are bereaved is very important. You do not need to have all the right answers or insight—you just need to *be* there. If you do not know what to say, silence is fine; do not try to force out words just to fill the void. Go to their home. Call them. Send flowers or a card. Tell them you are praying for them and that you love them. Write down scriptures for them that give comfort. Reassure them that they can live through their grief and that people will be there for them. Allow them to express their intense emotions and feelings without overreacting to them (unless you feel their behaviors are harmful to themselves or others). Attend wakes and funerals (more will be said in chapter 12 about this). Give affection when appropriate—a genuine hug can mean a lot.

Listen

Listen, listen, listen. "Everyone should be quick to listen, slow to speak and slow to become angry" (James 1:19). If most people would follow James's advice there could be a lot less grief in grief. The following are some guidelines that can help you be a better listener for those who are bereaved:

- Do not respond by giving advice or suggestions, especially while they are describing things to you.

- Do not interrupt to point out the positive side of things.

- Do not begin to share your own personal experiences or compare their loss with your loss or this death with other deaths while they are telling their story.

- Do not analyze the situation or begin to give your insight while they are telling their story.

- Do not try to fix their situation for them.

The bereaved will know if you are really there to help if you listen to them. You must learn to be able to listen to their story and endure their pain. To share their pain and be silent is one of the most important things you can do. Also, be "slow to speak" by thinking before you speak. Christians, like everyone else, can say some very insensitive and hurtful things. Use the listening guidelines above to help shape your thoughts and words to the bereaved. The intention of these guidelines is not to keep you from speaking, but to help you respond in thoughtful ways such as asking questions or reframing their story for further comment. Your speech can be helpful and encouraging if you knew the deceased and can share personally about him. Memories and experiences can be comforting to the bereaved as they try to remember the deceased and the deceased's impact on others' lives.

Help with Practical Needs

In the same way, faith by itself, if it is not accompanied by action, is dead. (James 2:17)

Reach out to those who are bereaved with practical help. Be like Jesus: care about them and for them. With every death comes a multitude of practical needs that you can help with, such as certain funeral arrangements, meals, household chores, baby-sitting, grocery shopping, lawn mowing, etc. The best kind of help comes when you step in and *do something*, not when you tell them you are available. Do not assume that others—even their closest relationships—are taking care of everything. Others may not see the needs that you do. Make sure that you do this with sensitivity to family and friends by asking and communicating with them about things that need to be done. You may need to create a list of needs and find the people to meet them. However, be honest and do not make promises that you do not intend to keep; if you offer help in some way, complete the job.

One very specific task involves dealing with the personal belongings of the deceased. Encourage those who are grieving not to be rash in discarding or removing them too soon. They may need you to help box and store things that they can go through at a later time. Also, it is okay to support them by leaving things as they are and revisiting their decision at a later time.

Think in a Larger Context

Most people are part of a larger group of relationships such as their family, church, workplace or school. Effective helping of those who are grieving involves seeing this bigger picture of relationships. All too often, the advice given to the bereaved can be inconsiderate of other family members, even though it is sound advice. Therefore you can end up becoming a problem in the scheme of things rather than a help. For instance, with the funeral service, you might give input that contradicts what the family wants, and as a result, a number of family members may be upset with you.

Proverbs 17:27 says, "A man of knowledge uses words with restraint." Learn to be sensitive to the larger context and use wisdom as you find your role as one of the many helpers, not as "the" helper. Also, do not forget the husband, wife, children or other family members by just focusing on one griever. All those affected by the death are part of the picture, not just the one who seemed to have the strongest relationship with the deceased or the one you are the closest to. By attending to the surrounding family, you will usually help the bereaved individual as well.

Don't Be Caught off Guard

> The race is not to the swift
> or the battle to the strong…
> but time and chance happen to them all.
>
> Moreover, no man knows when his hour will come.
> (Ecclesiastes 9:11–12)

Death presents spiritual challenges that push the bereaved off balance for a while and can cause many to struggle spiritually in dealing with the loss. Many, including the "strong," might do worse spiritually after the death than before it. Also, you may find that many resort to old coping strategies to deal with the loss rather than the new ways they have learned as a Christian. They may seek comfort and escape in alcohol rather than in prayer, or seek isolation and anger rather than fellowship and help. This is a time that can actually turn out to be more challenging for you, the helper, because it will call upon you to be more patient, accepting, caring, loving and flexible than before. (See chapter 2 "Spiritual Notes" for more understanding of the emotional responses of the bereaved.)

Death has a way of exposing and testing our faith, our convictions and our view of God and life. The worldview of the bereaved may not be what they claimed it to be, or they may move in the direction of changing their view of God because of the death. Though this may be upsetting or offensive to you, you must be able to hang in there with them and not be quick to judge them. Remember that they are in mourning and they need you to stick with them and gently help them to stay connected with God, even as they wrestle anew with their beliefs about God, life, the church and the truth.

At an appropriate time, which will vary from person to person, follow up with the bereaved and talk, reexamine or study the Bible for answers to the questions and challenges they have in their relationship with God. You may be called upon to help them renew their faith or to wrestle through the difficult issues that they now face in their Christianity.

Use Wisdom with Spiritual Issues

The early days of grief are not the time for you to interrogate those who are grieving about their views on the spiritual status of those who have died. Let them initiate that discussion when they are ready to deal with it. Sometimes you may be caught off guard by questions such as, "Do you think my mother is in heaven?" The best response may be that this is a time for them to grieve the loss of their loved one and that you would be available to talk with them later regarding their question. This lets them know that you are willing to discuss the issue at some future point while refocusing them on the situation at hand.

Also, think long and hard before you offer advice about what the bereaved "should" or "should not" be doing. Your preferences or actions may well be different from theirs. Also, keep in mind that they may be part of families in which advice circulates quickly—so be mindful of spiritual opinions and advice that you give.

It is important to be wise about the difference between the death of a Christian and the death of a non-Christian. Knowing what the Scripture teaches about being in a "saved" relationship with God makes grieving especially difficult if a Christian is grieving over the death of a non-Christian. If you are helping the bereaved and this is an issue, make sure that you consider this difference and respond appropriately. Read chapters 1 to 3, which shed more light on this subject. Be sure to encourage and support the bereaved when there is no deathbed conversion. All too often Christians punish themselves because their parents, family members or friends didn't respond to God like others have in the last moments of their life. Help them understand that whether or not a loved one responded to God is not necessarily a reflection on their own spirituality, and it never depends completely on them. Even in instances when the bereaved could have done a better job with sharing their faith or the gospel, it is important to remember that every individual is personally responsible to seek and respond to God, aside from the help of others. Discussing this topic with someone requires prayer, thought, and for some Christians, a considerable amount of help.

Educate Yourself

This book lists numerous people, books and resources that can help you understand death and dying in a deeper way. Helping requires some learning. Death involves many diverse situations. Whether it be understanding the difference between the way that men and women grieve or the complications of different deaths, God can broaden our understanding and in doing so, make us better helpers for the bereaved. At the same time, don't worry about being "the most educated helper" for the deceased. Be humble. Jesus calls us to give and help because we are Christians—not because we have a background in counseling. Last, be aware that as with any other subject there are poor resources on grief as well as good. The bibliography in this book will connect you with many who have been involved in working with death and mourning for years. I would suggest using them as a guide to further learning.

Prepare Yourself

Each heart knows its own bitterness. (Proverbs 14:10)

Grief is intense. It is possible that you will see more intense emotions than you have ever seen before. You may never have seen someone wail in the throes of grief. If it happens, don't overreact to it. Let the person know it is okay to cry, talk, cry again, talk again and that what they are going through is normal for grief. Do not try to restrain their emotions, especially if you do so only because you are uncomfortable. Read chapters 1 and 2 to educate yourself about the normal grief responses to loss. Also, be prepared for the long journey ahead. Helping someone who is grieving will take days, months, even years;

do not be frightened away by the process. Count the cost and make the decision to help all the way.

Watch for Warning Signs

Be attentive to how the bereaved person is doing. There are warning signs for those who are not handling things well. The following grief signs may warrant the bereaved getting professional help:

- *Excessive emotion*—guilt beyond what was done or not done regarding the deceased; anger which borders on alienation and revenge; depression that continues over time; anxiety that continually "works up" the person

- *Substance abuse*—excessive use of alcohol, drugs or medications to escape the loss

- *Suicidal thinking*—making statements regarding the hopelessness of life, the extreme desire to see the deceased again, or life not worth living without the deceased

- *Physical or psychological signs*—physical: any symptom that could possibly threaten the person's health; psychological: an inability to function at work or at routine chores

Difficult Days

Do not be taken aback by moodiness, crying, irritability or other emotions in those who are mourning on or around significant days or times connected with the death. Experience in working with the bereaved has shown that television commercials, smells, music, places and other things may easily trigger remembrances of the deceased and invite emotional reactions. In the same way, mothers who have lost children can have intense feelings and reactions around births or in the presence of other children. You can help by being sensitive to these times and places and by encouraging others to do the same.

Remind Them of God

> God has said,
>   "Never will I leave you;
>   never will I forsake you." (Hebrews 13:5)

By your love, words and actions, keep God close to them. Even when there is no response, stay alongside them. In time those who are grieving will appreciate and rely on the help and spiritual support that God and you bring to sustain them through grief.

Respect Cultural Differences

Paul challenges all of us by his heart to be "all things to all men" (1 Corinthians 9:22). Since Christians live all over the world and are part of every culture, we will continue to need to be open to learning about others' backgrounds. This will mean some work and searching the Scriptures on everyone's part to stay righteous and unified and to not let cultural differences or traditions keep us from meeting needs and supporting others in time of grief and mourning. This is discussed further in the appendix "Multicultural Mourning."

Be Open to Learning and Changing

Jesus often found himself responding to requests from socially stigmatized individuals such as lepers, prostitutes and

Samaritans. He was not swayed by how society viewed people, but loved people and reached out to them, meeting their needs. Deaths such as suicide, AIDS and homicide can test our hearts concerning our views of people. Like Jesus, we can find ourselves in the middle of deaths that carry some degree of social stigma and being asked to respond. Search your heart and deal honestly with any attitudes, viewpoints or feelings about these types of deaths that would keep you from being like Jesus and helping.

Helping Later in Mourning

Listening Later

Months after a death, those who are bereaved will need a different type of help. Very often they need to begin to listen to others. You can offer perspective to the bereaved on where you think they are and how you think they are doing. They may call upon you to help work through spiritual or life issues with them or to determine what the meaning in all of it has been. This should be handled sensitively and with good counsel and advice from others. An example of how *not* to handle such discussions would be to unload on them opinions about their grieving that you have stored up for the last several months, just waiting for the right time to tell them. This could close the door on any opportunity you might have to help.

Offer appropriate help by identifying for them certain continuing behaviors (fighting, arguing, restlessness and more) or emotions (anger or depression) that need attention. For instance, if a married couple is having difficulty in their relationship after the death of their child because they are not listening to each other, you might need to point this out to them.

You might need to help them with any unresolved issues that the death surfaced. Some examples are talking through things or finding practical ways of solving problems such as gathering information about the death or coming up with a working plan to deal with the remaining debt from the medical care the deceased received. Situations like these may need to be addressed in order for the bereaved to move on.

In addition you may feel a need to encourage them to seek specific help, professional help if necessary, especially if you feel that they are stuck at some point regarding the death. Also, encourage good health and respite. You can help by encouraging them to get rest, exercise and any mental breaks they need. These can help them to be renewed, refreshed and ready to deal with the day-to-day challenges that grief brings.

Be an Advocate

You can help find resources for the bereaved if they need them, such as counseling, government agencies, lawyers, doctors and financial counselors. Keep in mind the secondary losses that can occur with deaths: loss of homes, incomes and more. They may need assistance, along with encouragement, in addressing the new situations (such as employment or daycare, for example) thrust upon them by the death.

Be Consistent

> Many a man claims to have unfailing love,
>   but a faithful man who can find? (Proverbs 20:6)

One of the things those who are grieving need most is for you to *stay* alongside them. Too many have felt the help only for a short time after the funeral and then are left alone. They need your friendship more than ever as they get further down the path of mourning. Continue to listen and be there for them even if it just means a card or a phone call that says, "I love you."

Use Wisdom

As the bereaved work through mourning further, you need to be wise about encouraging them to pursue new ventures such as a dating relationship. Oftentimes our desires for the bereaved can overrun what they are feeling or are capable of emotionally handling at the moment, causing them to make hasty decisions. For instance, there is mounting evidence that shows children have a more difficult time mourning the loss of a parent if the surviving parent remarries within a year. In general, I believe that following a difficult loss it is wise to give a person time to adjust to life without the deceased before encouraging certain activities.

Remembrance

Support the efforts of the bereaved to remember their loved ones. Our society has very few rituals for remembering the dead, and this can inhibit some from openly creating a meaningful ritual that helps them to keep the memory of their loved ones alive. You can encourage their desire to create a memory book, have an honoring on a special day, plant a tree, or other ideas that help them keep a healthy connection to the deceased. At the same time, you can help them prepare for difficult times such as holidays (Christmas, Father's Day, Mother's Day, for example), special personal times and anniversaries that can be especially painful. Encourage them to think through a plan ahead of time for those days. However, remember it is just a plan. Do not hold them to a set of expectations that if not met becomes in their minds a failure. It may be overwhelming enough to them just to make a plan.

Helping with Child Bereavement

A brief word is included here on how children experience grief so that you will better understand their situations and be more equipped to help them. Sandra Fox, in her book *Good Grief* talks about four tasks that children need to accomplish in grieving.

- *Understanding*—this is how children make sense of the loss. Children experience loss differently at different developmental levels. Younger children may not view death as permanent or irreversible, but as they get older they will come to understand that death is irreversible, universal and nonfunctional. "Irreversible," meaning that once you are dead, you cannot be made alive again. "Universal" means that all things eventually die. "Nonfunctional" is defined as the ending of everything about the person that made them alive.

- *Grieving*—children will experience the same reactions to loss that adults do: physically, socially, psychologically and spiritually. Their grief needs to be acknowledged, respected and responded to appropriately according to their developmental level.

- *Commemorating*—children need to commemorate the death in concrete and meaningful ways.

- *Going On*—children need to redefine the relationship over time.[1]

Children may express their grief in many ways. Physically: they may experience different pains. Stomachaches are a common symptom. They may not feel like eating at times. They may begin wetting the bed, not having done so before. They may cry at any time and place. Socially: they may pull back from people, or they may do the opposite and act out against others. Psychologically: they may talk about their loved one over and over again, often in an idealized way. They dream about them or feel that they sense them around them. They may have nightmares, fears of abandonment, and trouble sleeping. They may have trouble concentrating on things such as homework. Spiritually: they may have questions about topics such as heaven, death or pain. They may seek ways to connect with their loved one. These are normal ways children express their grief, and we must be careful to recognize them as grievers no less than we do adults. Listed below are some general ways to help bereaved children.

Let Them Mourn

Children have the capacity to grieve and mourn, usually earlier than you might think. If you are not aware of this, you can easily forget and dismiss children from the mourning process. They react the most to the separation that death brings. Their grief is like adults' in that it can vary in duration and intensity. Children are best helped by allowing them to express their grief. Also, siblings mourning siblings should be recognized and helped. It can be too easy to focus on the surviving parent and marginalize or worse yet ignore the grief of the surviving sibling(s).

The Funeral

Children who are capable of responding should be given the choice of attending the wake, funeral and burial. Younger children will probably need the parent to help decide whether attendance is appropriate or not. This choice should be made after being given a description (age appropriate) of the event, sights, sounds, smells and emotions they may encounter. Information and preparation are the important elements here. Do not have children do things they are not comfortable with, such as touch or kiss the deceased; these forced actions can traumatize a child. Studies show that children who are prepared and allowed to participate in the funeral activities continue to have a positive view of them later on. So as much as possible it is good to include them in the funeral experience and other rituals that memorialize the deceased.

Adequate Information

Give children information about the death (such as the cause) that is clear, understandable and age appropriate. This will minimize their imagining situations or fabricating a story because of the lack of real information.

Reassurance

Following the death, children need to know they will be given support, nurturing and continuity. Support is felt "when the parent can function as a teacher and guide, providing feedback and encouragement about the child's feelings and behavior...."[2] Being a nurturing parent is not just providing the essentials of food, clothing and shelter, but being able to listen and respond to the children's emotional needs.

Also, children need to know that they are not to blame for the death whether by something they did or did not do, said or did not say. Younger children can often think that they have control over things by wishing, thinking or saying something.

This is a factor of their developmental age. Communicating with them about the death can be one way to work through this type of fantasy or magical thinking. Also, there are numerous books that provide other ways to help work through such unfounded guilt.

Maintain Boundaries

Continuity is extremely important—children should know that despite the fact that things have changed, the family will go on. For example, consistent discipline and routines should be maintained after a death (as best as circumstances allow). The tendency is to relax the rules when actually the need is to keep up the familiar rules. Children feel cared for when they know things are going to continue the way they were before the death.

Listening

Just as adults need someone to listen to them, so do children. They also need someone to answer their newfound questions about death—even those that may seem strange to adults, such as, "Will Grandpa go to the bathroom in heaven?" or as they look at the body in the casket, "Where are her feet?" Teens may have a difficult time explaining the loss of a parent to their friends. They may require time and attention to help them find ways to express their own grief as well as to communicate it to others. Books on children's grief can help with answering many of the questions that children and teens may have.

Validation of Feelings

Respect and acknowledge the children's feelings. Do not tell them to get over their grieving or that they are not grieving enough or to stop it just because it makes you uncomfortable. Remember, they are children and they deal with grief in their own way and at their own pace. For instance, playing can be a way that they take a break from grief, or it may be a way that helps them to make sense of death.

Overwhelming Feelings

Intense feelings can come to children as well. Help by allowing them to release their feelings in a healthy way and by giving them creative ways to express them, such as through drama, music, art, clay sculpting, painting or writing.

Grief Modeled

One way adults can help children is by modeling grief appropriately: discussing the deceased, reliving memories, talking of the positive and negative times and showing emotions.

Remembrance

Children need the support and the opportunity to remember the deceased during the rest of their lives. As they grow up, children will continue to think about, review and ask questions about their relationship with a deceased parent. Pictures, letters, videos and other things will help them as they continue to redefine their relationship to the deceased for years to come.

Red Flags

There are numerous indicators that should alert us to the fact that children are not handling grief well. First, refer to those listed at the beginning of the chapter. I would also add to those the following: academic failure or overachievement, dramatic shift in attitude or personality, eating disorders, fighting, inappropriate sexual behavior and legal trouble. These behaviors should alert us to the possibility that a bereaved child is not doing well and that professional help may be required.

Helping the Suicide Survivor

The following list of suggestions gives some direction and advice for helping suicide survivors.[3] It is important to read through the chapters on loss, grief and mourning prior to reading these suggestions so that you have a basic understanding of the normal grieving and mourning reactions and process.

Get Help!

Urge them to get help from suicide groups or personal counseling. There are specific issues that follow death by suicide that should be addressed early if possible.

Unrealistic Guilt

Survivors may feel guilty for not knowing in advance that the suicide was coming. At an appropriate time discuss these types of feelings and let the person know that they are natural and normal struggles. Help them understand where necessary that they are not able to control others' lives and are not responsible for the choices others make. They also need to know that the feeling of relief in some suicide situations (for example, suicide after a long bout with depression) is a common grief reaction.

Temptation to Isolation

Try not to let them isolate themselves due to the stigma that comes with suicide. Help them not to give in to the urge to stay apart from people and not to face them.

Unfinished Business

Help the survivor deal with any unfinished business with the deceased. Sudden death always creates difficulty in resolving old or existing situations. It does not allow the time to talk through the issues of life or resolve prior problems that, when dealt with, ease some of the pain of separation and make the transition easier.

Funeral Rites or Memorials

Survivors still need to grieve and mourn their loss, no matter how society views it. They have lost a loved one and need to have a time of remembrance that allows them to say goodbye and continue with living. The more they are able to have normal ways of grieving, the better the chance of their own adjustment to the loss in the mourning process.

Calm Fears About Heredity

Some may have the irrational fear that suicide is hereditary. They might fear that more family members will do the same thing, and the resulting anticipatory grief can give them extra emotional weight to carry. Help them calm those unfounded fears.

Give to Them

Don't pull back from those who are trying to put their emotional world in order after a suicide. They will need assistance and support in all the normal ways, and they may need help for legal, medical and insurance situations that can be even more challenging in a suicide death.

Refer When Needed

Sometimes the best way to encourage a suicide survivor is to help the person find local support groups for survivors. There is great comfort and camaraderie as one survivor talks to another. Check the resource section in the back of this book for suggestions.

Difficult decisions, intense emotions and new situations are often thrust upon us as we strive to help those who are hurting. Proverbs says, "A friend loves at all times, and a brother is born for adversity" (Proverbs 17:17). As the apostle Paul wrote, "Carry each other's burdens, and in this way you will fulfill the law of Christ" (Galatians 6:2). God is clear that Christians are meant to play a part in helping others through tough times. We must respond to the suffering with a heart of compassion, empathy, deep love and patience. We need to be willing to change what we need to, in order to better meet others' needs. When we pick up and carry their burden as far as they need us to, we truly fulfill the law of Christ.

When my mom died, I remember feeling great gratitude for the smallest tokens of kindness. For example: my dad, brother and I returned home with Mom's cremains, and some friends of his (theirs) were waiting for him, and his neighbor (78-year-old WWII bomber pilot) across the street shoveled his driveway after we got home. I simply cannot tell you how grateful I felt.

—Tom

7
To the Dying

Tom was a middle-aged professional man, married with kids. He was active in his church and loved his family. He began having problems over a period of time, but the doctors could never pinpoint a specific disease. After a number of years, there were other symptoms, and cancer was at last identified.

The news was devastating to his family, friends and church. All of a sudden his whole world had changed. He went from being in the prime of his life to facing a life expectancy of several years and a whole new routine consisting of hospital visits and treatments. His job was in jeopardy and he wondered if his finances could bear the strain of this unpredictable disease. In time spiritual issues became more pressing, not that the hospital and drug routines lessened, but the need to find some meaning for what was happening to him grew stronger.

On several occasions, Tom spoke with me about challenges he was feeling. In the beginning, we talked about the difficulty of facing the disease, his changing world and how he and others were coping. Later we spoke about what he was learning through all of it. He shared in tears about the things that now made his life more difficult, such as people not understanding his situation, not being able to do things with his son and the loss of his physical stamina and energy. Terminal cancer can take a person down some very unpleasant paths. For example, Tom would spend one day planning

139

some remarkable ways to prepare his family for a future without him and on the very next day would exhaustedly say, "I wish I would just go on and die."

Toward the end of his battle, he could say with the apostle Paul, "Though outwardly we are wasting away, yet inwardly we are being renewed day by day" (2 Corinthians 4:16). When all was said and done, this was Tom—he grew stronger spiritually as his body continued to falter. His focus began to sharpen on what truly mattered in life: his relationship with God and relationships with his family and friends. He was a constant encouragement to me till the end. After he died I went back through the notes I had taken during our conversations and found something that summed up Tom's perspective on his impending death. It read, "I know that the only way for me to get into heaven is by grace...and that is why I am at peace with dying."

If you are facing a terminal illness I hope this chapter helps you. I have chosen several broad categories to help frame our discussion of the challenges facing you.

Physical Changes

You, as you know already, are facing a whole new world physically. Whether cancer, ALS (otherwise known as Lou Gehrig's disease) or other terminal disease, you will experience many different physical changes. You may face a host of new medical treatments and regimens, such as surgery, chemotherapy, radiation, bone marrow transplants, MRIs, PET scans, ultrasounds, CAT scans, X rays or some combination of these. You may be given drugs to fight pain, drugs to fight infection, drugs to induce sleep and drugs to help with the side effects of all the other drugs you are taking. You can go quickly from being relatively healthy to becoming a very sick person. Sickness can come from the disease or from the treatments. The physically strong may become weak after major surgery. Fatigue can be a telling sign that your body is changing, and even climbing the stairs can be a chore. Pain is a new challenge. Before, pain may have been a temporary problem due to something minor like a cut or bruise, but now pain is a permanent resident in your body. Though it can be managed and made bearable, it is there and is a constant reminder of the affliction.

On a practical level, if you know you are dying, you will face decisions about your physical situation. You will have to decide whether to receive treatment or not. You will have to make decisions about your care at the time of death. Only you will know how you feel and what you are capable of doing physically. You will know better than anyone else the spiritual issues that are foremost on your heart as time progresses. In the end you must decide what you want to have done. It is your life and death, not that of others.

However, as a Christian, you need to show humility (as difficult as this may seem) in making your decisions. For instance, you may know that you do not want to suffer through a particular type of treatment when others are saying you should. You may feel that it is your body and this is the way you want it, case closed; but you must also listen to those who are affected by your decision. They may be pushing for the treatment because they want more time with you and know that if you decide not to take it, your life may be shortened. When all is said and done, you may decide not to have the treatment, but the people who care about you want to be heard and considered before you make the decision. By listening you learn things that may influence your decision-making later on or that reveal the need for specific actions such as a family talk, forgiveness toward particular people, unresolved feelings about others and more.

Time

Right from the beginning time is a big issue. "How long?" becomes the question, with others right behind it: "Will I have time to finish things I want to accomplish?" "Will I be able to see my daughter married?" "Will I be around long enough for my children to become Christians?" Life becomes a race in which every second counts. Time becomes the ruler by which life is now measured. Suddenly, life is short, it is "a mist that appears for a little while and then vanishes" (James 4:14). Not that a Christian would not have understood the brevity of life before, but dying brings this reality home in a sobering way. The prognosis of time may cause you to reconsider your life plans. You may find yourself changing your goals, dreams, projects, spiritual commitment or general attitude about life. How you use the time remaining may be a constant challenge to your thinking and scheduling. Situations like a remission can be encouraging as far as your outlook is concerned, but difficult as far as planning for the future. As a result, your life plans may change over and over again.

The process of dying can generally be described in three distinguishable periods of time:

1. *The Acute Phase*—when you receive your initial diagnosis. Reactions may vary and include emotions such as panic, denial, anxiety, depression and anger. They

may vary based on the status of your illness and available treatment options.

2. *The Chronic Phase*—when life becomes a gradual process of living and dying. This is when you get caught between your desire to be treated like a "normal" person and the fact that you are actually dying. It is a time when honesty and communication are important and isolation is harmful. Other situations that come to the forefront are financial concerns and expenses, insurance issues and paperwork, work capacity and options, new medical regimens and treatments, ongoing family adaptation to the disease, and spiritual capabilities and concerns.

3. *The Terminal Phase*—when you begin to respond to internal signals of impending death. You may begin to withdraw from activities outside the circle of your important relationships, resign yourself to a chosen approach to the end of your life or continue the fight against your disease in a new way. It may be that cure-based intervention has reached a point of futility or that financial costs now exceed any real physical long-term rewards. Also, spiritual issues may be resolved at this stage, as you prepare to say good-bye.[1]

Emotions

You will probably find that the initial diagnosis is one of the most difficult times in your experience. It opened a door to a world that you were not anticipating and one that you were not necessarily prepared for. Diagnosis casts a shadow of uncertainty over everything. It sets off numerous emotions

and responses such as denial, fear, sadness, anger, hopelessness, anxiety and depression. These emotions are a response
to the grief that you are experiencing as you are confronted
with the eventual loss of your life. These losses and your
resulting grief and emotions are probably the greatest challenges you will deal with day to day.

Very often the hospital setting may add to your emotional
discomfort as a result of treatment routines and other regimens. Also, the way in which other people respond to your situation can bring about undue emotional distress. You may
become anxious about how your family or friends might
respond or fearful that your job could be in jeopardy if you feel
that due to your illness you will not be able to perform up to
your capabilities.

Practically speaking, talking is key during this time. It can
make a big difference for you to have someone to talk with
consistently. Talking allows you to process information, think
out loud about decisions, and express emotions. Talking may
not be easy for you. It may be difficult to start expressing how
dying is affecting you physically, emotionally and spiritually.
And it may take time for you to learn how to identify what you
are feeling and thinking and then be able to share it with
someone. You may never have had a conversation about your
death with anyone, so it is understandable that you may have
difficulty discussing it openly with many. This is okay initially,
but I would encourage you to start talking as soon as possible.

Also, you may get angry when others want you to see your
dying their way. In other words, you are going to die and they
want you to start preparing for it. Do not let this kind of situation separate you from people or keep you from talking. Do
your best to be patient with others and to try to explain your

view of things. But be open to hearing the concerns of others, especially medical personnel, even though you may not agree with their opinions at that particular moment. There must be willingness on everyone's part to listen to each other and work together as you start to come to grips with your situation. Keep in mind that this can be a first-time experience for all involved, and initially most people are not prepared to deal with it.

Spiritual conversations may be difficult to initiate and sustain. At first you may find that your emotions are directed at God and you are not sure how to handle them. This is when talking to a spiritually mature person helps. Such a person will allow you to raise questions and issues that require spiritual answers, not medical ones. You will need to become comfortable saying the things that go through your mind. This may be difficult if you feel that a Christian should not question God or his will. However, as the book of Job points out, God is fine with the questioning, but he does want you to hear his reply when it is time. Staying continually open about what you are feeling and thinking can help you work things through as you go instead of letting them pile up, which can cause bad attitudes and a hardened heart. Also, people will naturally want to understand how you are thinking spiritually as you get closer to death. They might ask you questions about how you lived your life and whether you have any unfinished business to work through, such as attitudes or feelings toward anyone. They might talk with you about your understanding of heaven. Sometimes these questions are difficult to hear. Be honest about how the questions affect you, and trust that others care about you and ultimately want the best for you.

Relationships

You may face challenges with many relationships. You may at first feel as if you have become a "sick" person and people have pulled back from you or completely abandoned you. This may cause you a great deal of emotional pain and hurt, as if dealing with the disease itself were not tough enough. However, there is no way around it: dying is hard on friends and family. The challenges of time, energy, medical appointments, sickness, treatments and new errands can put a strain on your close relationships, making the time for emotional connections even harder to find. As family and friends become your "caregivers," relationships can suffer if they are not worked at. You must also now connect with a host of new people, such as nurses, hospice workers, doctors and therapists. All of these new connections require withdrawals of your physical and emotional energy that now seem to be in short supply. Be patient with people. Everyone is adjusting. Do your best to share what is happening to you and attempt to ask what is happening for them. You will continue to need your close relationships alongside you as you fight this battle.

Coping

Managing the loss, grief and emotion of dying is a constant challenge. Typically, you will rely on ways of coping that work for you as you face the challenges of your disease. I have listed below five ways of coping with dying. It may be important for you to look through them and acknowledge if any of them apply to you. If you can identify your tendency or tendencies, it is important to communicate these to the people who are engaged in this fight with you. Understanding your approach and thinking will help them to work with you in a better way.

1. Denial

You are not ready to accept a particular outcome and instead seek to dwell on certain other possibilities. This may not be wrong, due to the fact that faced with the certainty of your situation, you may not be emotionally capable at the time to deal with or respond to it. This can be a viable coping mechanism for you at certain times but not continually. If you continually ignore certain situations or discussions, you may leave supporting people in a quandary as to how best to meet your needs. You may also delay spiritual conversations that need to take place or end-of-life issues that need to be specified.

2. Faith

You choose to face your situation with a belief in God and the promise of an afterlife (see the following "Spiritual Notes" section and chapter 4). You view your encounter with death in a faithful way, and in your suffering you draw meaning from the Bible. A good admonition here might be from Romans where Paul says about Abraham that even with great faith he "faced the fact" (Romans 4:19), which helps us understand that often there are facts to be considered. Even if you are at peace with whatever God allows, you need to make sure to talk about facts that need to be faced: difficult days ahead, funeral arrangements, alternative or additional treatment, requests from family or friends, a will, etc. This is not to take away from your faith but to remind you that others may be wrestling with your situation in different ways, and it is important to address their concerns.

3. Fight

You may see your disease as "the enemy" that must be fought on all fronts. It has invaded your body and must be attacked in every way possible: physically, emotionally, mentally and spiritually. As Lance Armstrong once said regarding his cancer, "You picked the wrong guy."[2] I write in chapter 4 that I believe that God is for life. I would encourage you to fight your battle with the disease if possible. You do not know in what ways God will help you in your situation. I have a friend who has been battling cancer for over three years in many different ways, and he needs my support and encouragement to continue on. His intent is to save others and glorify God with what time he has. I say Amen! I know you are not dead but alive, and I would encourage you to fully live every moment you have on this earth. Make sure however that you are honest in your fight. You need to acknowledge realities (declining prognosis, failed medical treatment, etc.) and be open to discussion and advice from others who love and care for you.

4. Problem Solve

You look at your life, now changed because of disease, as an ongoing set of problems to be solved or worked on. You may be working on a number of projects that you feel require attention before you die. The disease itself can become a project that involves researching everything known about it and talking shop with doctors and others. You cope by setting goals you want to accomplish and then using available time and energy to work toward them, even over and above that which the disease requires of you physically or emotionally. This way of coping is like all the others: it has a good side and another side that might not be so good. The good side is that you choose to focus on projects that can mean a lot to people around you, such as letters, videos, conversations, trips, finances, etc. Spiritually, you can help ease others' eventual journey through mourning by things you do before your death. For instance, helping coordinate financial arrangements for your family before death can help by eliminating or making easier situations that could complicate their life after your death, thus making mourning more difficult. On the other hand, you can become so focused on projects that you lose sight of all else. It may help you face death easier, but it may make things extremely difficult for others who want to have quality time with you.

5. Acceptance/Resignation

You may find yourself in a position of submitting to the evident end of your life. This may come after a long battle with your disease or after receiving a shorter prognosis regarding your situation than was originally told you. You either make a "decision of faith" to stop fighting and use the time at hand to prepare for the end, or you make a "decision of fatigue" due to the mental and physical strain of the disease. Your decision might be a combination of the two. No matter which decision is true for you, you need to feel that acceptance is okay. You are the one who has to decide how far and long you can go. In the end only you will truly know the full extent of the disease working against you. You will need to communicate this to those around you so they can accept your decision and work to support you in the time you have left.

Wherever you find yourself in this process of coping, I would like to encourage you with the words of Paul, who says,

"...whether by life or death. For to me, to live is Christ and to die is gain" (Philippians 1:20–21). Be at peace with your decision. Know that you are loved and appreciated. Do what you are capable of doing to make the end of your life the best possible transition for all involved.

Spiritual Notes

Meaning and Purpose

The most challenging questions for you are much the same as those the bereaved face: "Why?" and/or "Why me?" I have listed a few suggestions below that may help in your search for answers.

- Read chapters 3 and 4.

- Seek help from God: look for examples in the Bible that can give you insight about your situation. Remember what Paul says in 2 Corinthians 12:9:

  "My grace is sufficient for you, for my power is made perfect in weakness." Therefore I will boast all the more gladly about my weaknesses, so that Christ's power may rest on me.

- Pray that God will give you answers and that he will keep your heart soft. Romans 8:28 says, "And we know that in all things God works for the good of those who love him...." To the very end God is working for your good, even though there will be times when it may not feel like it. God will help you deal with the issues facing you if you will continue to seek help from others and from him.

- Get help from others who are going through the same experience you are and who can share their convictions with you.

- Don't let yourself get discouraged and quit. God knows the difficulty you are facing. His grace encourages you to rely on him to help you both face and work through things such as character issues, family dynamics, physical challenges and more.

- Live! See this as a time to deepen your relationship with God and others. Learn to use your remaining time to accomplish all you can and to draw closer to God and your family and friends.

Attitude

What kind of attitude will you have about dying? Will it be like Paul's attitude: "For to me, to live is Christ and to die is gain" (Philippians 1:21)? It is important to determine early on that you will have a spiritual attitude about dying. You may ask, "What is the attitude I'm supposed to have?" Paul follows up his first statement by saying, "Your attitude should be the same as that of Christ Jesus" (Philippians 2:5). Paul is trying to help, not to overwhelm, as he points to the example of Jesus—an example that can help you with dying as well as with living.

Jesus faced death himself and left us an example to follow. Hebrews describes his experience and attitude in different ways: he "suffered death," he was made "perfect through suffering," he shared in our "humanity," he is able "to sympathize with our weaknesses" and "he learned obedience from what he suffered" (Hebrews 2:9–10, 14; 4:15; 5:8).

To begin, I would say that Jesus had a teachable attitude. He was humble and "learned" as he suffered. He learned how to deal with the fact that he was going to die and how to have God's attitude about it. The same goes for you—God must be the greatest influence on you in facing dying. He must be able to teach you through people like Paul, who confronted death as gain and ultimately viewed the time he had left as an opportunity to serve Jesus Christ. Being teachable also means being open to others' advice or opinions about your approach to death. Humility can help you hear both God and others as you learn to take on the challenge of dying.

Second, God's character must become your character. As you see in the passages from Hebrews cited above, character is developed in the face of suffering (see also Romans 5:3–4). Endurance, integrity, courage, dignity, patience and other traits must find their place in your dying. Endurance may manifest itself in your acceptance of the fact that it will be a struggle right to the end. Remember what Lance Armstrong said about his fight against cancer and what it taught him about being meant for the long, hard climb. You, too, will need to have the attitude that you can make it through suffering and dying. Having the courage to cry, to laugh, to wince in pain, to say no, to strengthen others, to go to another appointment, or to pray when you don't feel like it. Job had a sense of integrity that refused to let go of God even when everything else said to do so. Your battle will be to have this same kind of integrity. With the help of God and those around you, you can find and maintain a godly attitude to the end. (Always realize that confession of a sinful attitude is a part of having spiritual integrity, and never forget that it is God's grace that saves you.)

Gifts

Dying will be work. It will be work to pray with your kids, to make a video for them for later, to talk to your friends, to share about your life with others, to write letters, to have dinner with people you love, and more. It will be work to face the endless rounds of doctor visits, treatments, phone calls and other medical routines. It will be work to...you already know what I mean. I want to encourage you by telling you that the gifts you leave behind for those you love are worth it—even though creating those gifts take work. Going to doctors' appointments or continuing treatment that gives others more time with you, will be a golden gift to those who love you. It will be meaningful for someone to see that you pushed yourself to make it to their graduation or wedding, for example. If you do not achieve the "wished for" outcome or goal that you wanted, remember that your effort is a gift that will be long appreciated by others after you have died. Those who receive gifts will find that these gifts will help them recall your faith, love, hope, endurance and heart, which will strengthen them long after you are gone.

Paul reminded Timothy, as he viewed his impending death, of the spiritual gifts and truths that he had left to him, including his "teaching, [his] way of life, [his] purpose, faith, patience, love...[and] sufferings" (2 Timothy 3:10). Paul knew that after he died, these would help to sustain Timothy's faith. He understood the important role that these gifts would play and charged Timothy to "continue in what you have learned and have become convinced of," to "[fight] the good fight," "[finish] the race," "[keep] the faith" and receive "the crown" (2 Timothy 3:14, 4:7–8).

Honesty

Be honest with people and speak the truth in love (Ephesians 4:15). Communication while dying is extremely important. Dying creates all types of circumstances that require talking and more talking. You may have to be the one to initiate conversations, but do it. Above all, be honest. Tell people in a loving way the truth about you and how you are doing. Feel free to tell people you want to be considered alive not dead. Tell them that you are still a Christian and want to be expected to live that way even in the face of death. Tell people you want to keep your hope alive. Tell them you do not want them to back away. Tell them that you are going to participate in decisions about your care and comfort. Tell them what you do and do not want (see chapter 11 on decisions). Tell them you want them to be honest with you. Tell them that you need to express your emotions. Be honest because when you do, you keep Satan from gaining any foothold in your heart and from making dying more challenging than it already is.

Love

A Christian friend of mine who knows he is dying was asked if he thought about heaven at all. He replied that he saw it as a loving embrace from God, as if God were reaching down with these long arms and giving him a huge hug. In one way, this should describe the end of your life—that you will go from the love of those around you here to the love of God there.

Love is still a verb, however, which means that all parties involved must constantly work at it. Keep in mind that when people fail you or do not seem to understand your situation, they are learning to love you in a whole new circumstance. Give them the grace to learn to love you in the midst of situations that require something more from them. At the same time, remember that God also expects you to grow in your love during this time. For instance, if they do not complete all the chores exactly as you want them done or they are not available at a moment's notice, then you must learn to love them anyway.

Dying is a process that we are not "experts" in, and all of us will need to grow in our love for each other as we go through it. Patience, kindness, humility, selflessness, self-control, purity, happiness, trust, protection, hope and perseverance are some of the most difficult aspects of love to grow in as a Christian— but even more so in the face of ongoing suffering. Be advised however that if you do not love, then you open the door to bad attitudes, isolation, frustration, bitterness, resentment and more. Rather, we should have the attitude that the apostle John spoke about: "This is how we know what love is: Jesus Christ laid down his life for us. And we ought to lay down our lives for our brothers" and " let us love one another, for love comes from God" and "we love because he first loved us" (1 John 3:16; 4:7, 19). Faith will keep you inspired, hope will keep you persevering, but to the very end, love is the most excellent way.

Living with AIDS

The following suggestions are for those who have AIDS or are HIV positive.

- *Sharing information*—use good judgment when sharing about your situation with others. You may need to think through how and when information is made known. This can help you maintain a degree of confidentiality that's necessary for you to work through your particular situation and gather around you the support you will need.

- *Stay involved*—obviously alone time is important but stay involved. Talk to people, get out, stay in touch, find people who can listen to you and support you as you find your way through this challenging time.

- *Learn to talk*—get to the point that you can talk openly about your disease and let others know that you are comfortable doing so.

- *Deal with worry*—learn to identify things that can drain your energy and bring undue pressure on you. Take time to address these types of "worries" so that you prevent them from robbing you of valuable physical and emotional energy.

- *Take a break*—you need times (even in your mind) to step away from the challenges AIDS brings and allow yourself to breathe and be refreshed in some way. Communicate to others who can help you make this time happen.

- *Expand*—find other ways of coping. Consider other methods or expressions of thinking through your situation, such as music, writing, drama or art. These may lead you to new or additional ways of approaching and coping with your disease.

- *Take care of yourself*—this can be as simple as maintaining your physical appearance or finding relaxing activities to rest your mind. It also involves dealing with emotions such as anger and not allowing them to turn into destructive behaviors.

- *Attitude*—attempt to work toward an acceptance of your situation and find meaning in it.

- *Find an advocate*—identify someone who can and will listen to your feelings and thoughts and can help speak up for you. You will need others at times to bring issues to the table that you need help with. There will also be medical and insurance issues that you may need assistance with due to the state of your health.

- *Stay spiritually connected*—dying with any disease is spiritually challenging. But to die of a disease that has the social complications that AIDS has can be even more challenging. You must be determined to stay connected to God and the church. This means being open about the spiritual questions and thoughts that come up and initiating discussion about them. It means expressing your feelings in an honest way and allowing others to help you to find a way to deal with them.

- *Know your resources*—resources may be available to you in your local church as well as in your community and in the medical realm. You will need help with information and assistance in the variety of situations that you may encounter and in determining what options and alternatives are available to you.

- *Learn to grieve your losses*—read chapters 1, 2 and 3 to help you understand the process anyone goes through in dealing with losses.

- *Use your condition to save others*—whenever possible, allow your condition to open up the hearts of others. If you are a Christian living with AIDS, you will meet many new people in the process of dealing with it. Share your faith—take the opportunity to help someone else find God.

My Story
The Loss of My Wife
Ron Cicerchia

I married Jane Ellen Pattison of Davenport, Iowa, on January 13 of 1990. It was a wonderful evening ceremony complete with a string quartet in a candlelit New England church. It was everything Jane had dreamed her wedding would be, except for one detail. Six months earlier she had been diagnosed with an advanced form of ovarian cancer. The doctors presented us with a bleak prognosis. Depending on how well she responded to surgery and chemotherapy, Jane was expected to live between six months and a year. Despite this news we decided to make the most of whatever time we would have together. God blessed us not only with that one year but almost four. I am especially thankful I was able to be at Jane's side in our home as she took her last strained breath. She died just past midnight on November 16, 1993, three days after her thirty-ninth birthday. No more pain, no more tears, only a promise to meet again one day in eternity on the "North Corner of Glory" (Jane's directions).

It was hard to see Jane deteriorate physically over a period of several months before she died. When the end came, it brought me sadness and a sense of relief. Relief that Jane was no longer suffering, but also relief for me. The long fight was finally over. I remember a sense of numbness as I went through the preparations for the memorial service and the funeral. I didn't want to feel anything. That period immediately after Jane passed is a blur to me.

The activity helped to take my mind off the loss and the emptiness that I knew would come soon enough. Actually, I didn't
know what that emptiness would be like or when it would hit.
Would it totally overwhelm me? Would I be an emotional train
wreck for months...years? I was afraid of this unknown. I dreaded
the "G" word. Grief and mourning was a process I did not want to
experience.

God is faithful. I believe that with all my heart. His plan of salvation is the perfect response to this imperfect world. Even death
has no victory over our lives. Yet we grieve.

For a period of time I found comfort in keeping our home just the
way it was. I could sit and look around at all of the small touches
that were Jane. This helped to soften my sense of loss. But it soon
became obvious that I could not hold onto Jane like this. The
smells faded. The special touches got dusty. It was like water
flowing through my fingers. Jane was really gone. She wasn't
going to walk up the stairs and around the corner. I wasn't going
to hear her voice or feel her embrace in this life ever again. For a
while I cried every day.

Life has a way of marching on. Fall gives way to winter. Holidays
are always on time. I remember feeling so out of step. Everyone
around me had moved on, yet I was feeling the loss more than
ever. This was a hard time. For me that first year after Jane's
death brought the most intense waves of grief. I characterize that
year as the year of "firsts": the first Thanksgiving without Jane,
the first Christmas, the first wedding anniversary. There were

those awkward times when someone would ask about Jane not knowing she had passed away. Sometimes there were reminders that came out of the blue, triggering that deep sense of loss: a piece of mail addressed to Jane, checking off my marital status as widowed on an application, hearing a special song on the radio. This patchwork of emotion and memories was how I experienced grief. The intensity does lessen over time. I still tear up now and again, but that emptiness has been replaced with a sense of having loved and of having been loved in return.

I am thankful for the incredible group of family and friends who supported us over the entire time Jane was sick and beyond. There will always be a special place in my heart for each and every person who reached out in even the smallest way. For me, it wasn't important for someone to say just the right thing at just the right time. There were times when I didn't want to talk at all. It was great just to go out with friends and not discuss how I was doing. Other times I wanted to talk. I wanted to hear someone share their memories of Jane. I appreciated the people who didn't feel the need to force the conversation or try to relate to my loss. Being real and just being a friend is enough. Grief isn't something you have to fix. I have come to view it as a God-given process. Another example of how much God cares for us.

If there was a benefit to facing death over a prolonged period, it was the opportunity we had to talk about it. Not in that abstract "what if" kind of way, but in that real "when I'm gone" way. I did not particularly like those conversations at the time. I now realize what a gift they were. Jane told me she wanted me to remarry, to move on with my life, and above all to be happy. When I was ready, these things helped me to take the steps toward moving into that next chapter of my life. On March 16, 1996, I married the beautiful Melanie Storme Martel. Together we are raising our three equally beautiful daughters: Elizabeth, Marilisa, and Lauren.

8
Helping the Dying

Then they sat on the ground with him for seven days and seven nights. No one said a word to him, because they saw how great his suffering was.

Job 2:13

In August of 2002 I rode for the first time a two-day, 200-mile bicycle ride for the Dana-Farber Jimmy Fund. It was a fund-raiser called the Pan Mass Challenge (PMC) with the goal of raising money for the fight against cancer. More than 3,600 riders of all ages and backgrounds participated. There were a number of cancer survivors, but most were riders who had lost friends or family to cancer or who knew people fighting the battle currently. On the first day I rode wearing the PMC jersey, but on the second day, I rode with a jersey that had the names of my friends whom I was riding for written on it. It was a tremendously uplifting and emotional experience to be a part of such a community of people, including the volunteers as well as the riders.

Looking back on it, I see many parallels to helping those with cancer or other terminal conditions. First, you must ride your race and the dying must ride theirs. I can ride to raise money that helps in the fight against their disease. I can ride to encourage them, to tell them that they are cared about, and to say that I will suffer for them (even in a small way), but I cannot take their place. I can assist them, help them, support them and ride alongside them, but they must ride their own race. Generally, it is those of us who are helping who must face this hard truth. The dying understand it; they know that they must make the decisions, choose the paths and live with the results—not anyone else.

Second, as I rode along, I passed many riders, riding at different paces and in different ways. I thought about each name I had written on my jersey and how each had chosen to ride his or her own way. We who are helping have the privilege of riding alongside the dying, and we must learn to help by riding at the pace at which they are riding. This can be extremely frustrating to many, but essential to those who are dying. Remember, it is they who must listen to their bodies and minds to determine when they need assistance, support, courage, comfort, listening or quiet. We must be patient and not try to take over or tell them how to ride their own races.

Third, it will be an emotional ride for us as helpers, too. As I approached the finish line after two full days of riding I began to think of all of the friends whom I was riding for, and I began to cry. I did not expect to react that way, but I did. Helping the dying will be an emotional and life-changing ride too, and that is okay. Those who are dying mean a lot to us, and we will feel for them in many different ways and at many different times.

After I finished the ride I told myself I would do it again. I said this knowing two things: First, I like to ride and it was a great experience. Second, and most important, to ride is to help the dying. And helping the dying is one thing I want to continue to do.

Helping those who are dying has its obligations. It calls not only for a compassionate heart that is like Jesus' heart, but also for a commitment to follow through, similar to the actions of the Good Samaritan. Please make sure that you read chapter 7 addressed to those who are dying so that you will understand the reasons for the practical suggestions offered here.

If you picked up this book, you are almost certainly looking for help with issues related to dying. Obviously, there are people who will live for many years with chronic illnesses and other health challenges. Such people need our help and many of the principles discussed here certainly apply to anyone who lives with an illness. However, this chapter is concerned primarily with helping those who are closely approaching death, due to either a life-threatening illness or a terminal medical condition. The acute nature of imminent death brings its own particular challenges. In this chapter I will sometimes refer to "the dying" and at other times to "those living with illness." In either case, it is important to realize that we are talking about people who are still *living*, even if their life expectancy has been drastically shortened as a result of a terminal illness.

Practical Help

Pain Management

Those who are dying deal with different types of pain and varying degrees of it. Pain can be managed. No one should be living in constant unbearable pain. We should encourage anyone in this situation to seek help. People who resist because they have heard that "pain medicine knocks you out" need to be informed that medicine can be adjusted to maintain a reasonable quality of life, while not impairing the ability to function. Generally pain is managed by a prescribed drug regimen or another type of therapy. We may need to help them find resources for pain management if they are not on a regimen. Also, some people may be concerned about addiction to pain medication, especially if there has been substance abuse in their background. Charles Corr, author of *Death and Dying, Life and Living,* wrote,

> That addiction does not occur, even when strong narcotics are prescribed in high doses for dying persons, has been shown by well-established research (for example, Twycross, 1976) and should now be well known (Porter & Jick, 1980). This psychological "high" and subsequent craving for steadily escalating doses that characterize addiction are not found.[1]

Loss of Energy

Living with illness brings about a loss of energy. People who are sick may not feel like participating in everything they would like to. We can help them continue friendships and stay involved by doing such things as visiting them, bringing activities to them or fulfilling some of their obligations (with their permission). We need to respect their need to save their energy to participate in things they feel most urgent about or believe to be most necessary for them and their families.

Other Physical Losses

Be sensitive when making comments about physical features. For example, chemotherapy treatment can cause hair loss, and cancer can drastically reduce a person's weight. And we might also watch not "making comments" with our eyes when we look at the obvious changes.

Routines

We might need to help by providing rides to medical appointments and treatments or by helping with food shopping and preparation or house cleaning. And when we make a commitment to arrive at a certain time, we should do everything possible to be there when we say. Those of us who are able-bodied have no idea how the dying have to manage their rest, their medication and their meals in order to be ready to leave the house at a certain time. This is not a period of easy flexibility.

Advanced Stages of Dying

We might be called upon, especially if we are family members, to provide more than just help. We might be required to assist with physical care such as lifting, giving medication, bathing, toilet assistance and more, which can extend over long periods of time. These activities may call upon us to dig deeper in our heart to continually respond and assist with them. Those who do will be challenged by the task, but also will be blessed by getting to serve in this way. Remember that God sees and blesses our heart and service as well (Matthew 25:40). It also helps to remind ourselves of how much this kindness and careful attention would mean to us if we were the one in their situation.

Emotions

Working with people who are dying is very similar to helping bereaved people work through their loss and grief. We will need to listen and provide a safe place for them to talk and to be open. (It would be good to go back and review the chapters on loss and grief and on helping the bereaved.) Your presence and ability to listen will go a long way in helping since they have much to work through and sometimes very little time in which to do it.

Quality of Life

We might be called upon by those living with illness to help them evaluate their quality of life. We might become a sounding board for discussing their thoughts about their physical condition, relationships, activities, expectations, mental state and spiritual condition. These discussions may involve getting our input or perspective on decisions.

Affection

Touch and appropriate affection can lift people's spirits and let them know that we accept their condition and are not turned away by it. Jesus had a way of touching the sick and not only healing their illnesses, but healing them emotionally as well. There was surely a gasp from the crowd when he reached out and touched the man with leprosy in Matthew 8:3.

Control

People living with illness will strive to maintain as much control in their lives as possible. This is one way they cope with the day-to-day challenges. This may manifest itself in different ways, such as trying to maintain a full routine or schedule or in seeking to know everything possible about their disease and the various options regarding treatment. As helpers we need to know that this control is important in many ways. It keeps hope alive, tells them the progress of their disease, keeps the disease from becoming their life, and more. We can help and support them by allowing them to continue to make decisions about their situations. We can then support their decisions even if at times they are not the choices we would have made.

We need to allow them to do things for themselves as long as they are physically capable. We must be mindful, as helpers, of the desire to overprotect them. Remember that this is their life and they are the primary ones who have to live with the decisions they make about it.

There are times, however, when control needs to be discussed, such as when their physical capabilities decline and safety becomes an issue. Also, with factors like stronger medication and dementia, discussions must be had about what activities they are capable of continuing to do. This should be a sensitive discussion and one that is negotiated with them so that they feel they are still involved in directing their lives. If a discussion is not possible due to their condition, then there may come a time when decisions will have to be made for them. See chapter 11 for more on this subject.

Information

Be honest but wise in sharing information with the dying. Sometimes those who are dying may not have all the information about their situation and might try to obtain it from us. We need to be careful about responding to them. The best way may be to ask them what they already know. If we happen to know more than they do, then wisdom would dictate to encourage them to pursue, from family or medical personnel, more accurate information. If they have had a hard time getting it, then we can inquire of family as to the reason information is being withheld. We should not let ourselves get in a position of revealing information that others close to them have not communicated.

Also, we may ask, if we are family, "Do we tell them everything?" Once again, people have the right to know the truth about their situation. It is generally best to be honest with those who are dying, even children, unless they have made it very clear that they do not want to know anything. How to tell them and what to tell them are usually the greater concerns. If you are in this situation, here are some principles to keep in mind.

Get advice. Talk to others, pray, get help from other resources such as books and professionals.

Consider their character and personality. Think about how they generally deal with things and how they have coped with difficult information in the past. Watch them; their body language can tell you a lot about whether they are open to listening or if they do not want to hear any more.

Give it to them in doses. Most people do better when they receive information in small amounts at a time. You should not drop all the information on them at once, but give them part of it, and then ask them how much more they want to know. It is helpful at times to ask them to repeat what they heard you say so you know if they understand it or not. You need to be patient as they take it in and wait until they appear ready before proceeding with more—or stop if they have had enough for the moment. Sometimes they realize it is important for them to know their full situation if there are decisions to be made.

Leave diagnosis and prognosis to the professionals. Let the professionals do their job. If questions arise after the professionals have stated their cases, then you may comment, ask them questions or ask them for clarification. You must be careful not to discredit their doctors because this can hurt the trust they have placed in them to provide for their care.

Respect the context of family or friends. If you are a friend, you must not overstep your boundaries. Family systems need to be honored. If you feel that a sick or dying person's desires for information are being ignored, you need to speak to the family first, and then get any help and advice you might need to go on from there.

Also concerning information, people may need someone to do research for them regarding their disease. Sometimes due to the limitations of time and the nature of their disease, they may not be able to do this for themselves. Having this information helps them in making decisions about treatment and time. Others might not want to know about the disease; all the same, they need someone to do research for them and their families or friends so that when it comes time for decisions, the information is available for all to consider. At times, knowing this information—such as the purpose of a particular test—can save them unnecessary physical and mental stress.

Dignity

Those living with illness struggle with a loss of dignity. By their very nature, the physical aspects of disease—the sights, sounds and smells—can tend to reduce a person's sense of self-worth and self-esteem. We can help and support them in various ways. One way is to offer a spiritual perspective about their situation. They can lose sight of how much they mean to others, the inspiration they provide, the spiritual strength they show and the faith that calls others higher. We can encourage and remind them to see these things. Also, we can help them by encouraging them to complete projects that are important to them, such as taking trips they have always wanted to take or resolving conflicts, relationships or other issues before they die. These types of things can help them maintain their dignity right up to the end.

Preparations

We might be asked by the terminally ill to help with planning such things as the memorial or funeral service or financial arrangements. We should not be taken aback by this, but be encouraged that we can serve in these ways. If we feel confused or awkward about such things, we can get advice on how best to participate.

Isolation

Often, the process of disease can isolate people. We can help them to sustain their relationships, keeping them from becoming isolated. This can be achieved in various ways such as having a small group of friends to their home or arranging (with their permission) different activities such as a time of honoring, a fun event or a prayer time together.

Advocacy

Those living with illness will have to make many preparations before death. They often need a hand with locating resources to work through problems. They may need someone to call, advise, locate, represent and deliver paperwork or mail. We may be tempted to feel as if our time is too valuable to do these chores, but for those who get exhausted just by walking around the house, we can fulfill a great need.

Spiritual Help

Holding Up Their Arms

Disease presents a continual battle of working through changes and fighting the decline in health. It will challenge even the spiritually strongest people, as evidenced by the story of Job. During this journey, they need others to walk alongside them and to pull them along (see Ecclesiastes 4:9–12). This may require more of us than we imagine. It may mean long phone calls, many late-night talks, a constant sharing of scriptures that address their particular needs, being consistently present, and all the other things Christians do to take care of people they love. The challenge for us as helpers is to stay with it. We need to "be devoted to one another in brotherly love" (Romans 12:10). When our devotion is really tested, we will be tempted to let go, but we cannot! God knows what we are doing and will give us the strength to continue on if we ask him for it. Romans 12:12 continues, "Be...patient in affliction, faithful in prayer." We must pray to be patient in the middle of suffering. We are rendering to others an invaluable service that at times only God may see, but is necessary for them to keep fighting the daily battle of staying alive both spiritually and physically.

Daily Character

Listed below are some of the character issues that those who know they are dying must face on a daily basis. Supporting them involves helping them face these issues daily as a Christian should.

- *Emotions*—such as bitterness, resentment, anger and frustration. We need to listen, letting them express emotions. However, we should not rush to interpret and judge the content. Help them work through it, rather than overreact to it.

- *Purposelessness*—feeling useless, not knowing what role they are to fill now. We also need to assist them in finding a new spiritual role because everyone has a purpose, even up to the day they die.

- *Identity*—not being the people they used to be physically and not fulfilling the roles they used to. They must wrestle with the fact that things have changed due to illness, but that their identity is defined by who they are, not what they are able to do or not do.

- *Insecurity*—feeling forgotten by others who are going on with their lives or feeling isolated by their new lifestyle. We need to use these times of insecurity to sympathize with them, but also to give them vision (see Proverbs 27:17, 25:11). We need to get people around them (unless medically difficult) and get them around people, by calling them, having others call them, writing cards, having people accompany them places, and other ways. If at all possible we should stay with them all the way to the end.

- *Perception*—feeling like other people do not know what it is like; feeling like this is not fair and that others don't understand. Many times they will be right about what they perceive, but we must help them to have the right heart toward circumstances—not a bad attitude. We need to learn to have conversations that are not confrontational about these issues, but rather are conciliatory.

- *Vigilance*—keeping their spiritual wits about them, staying in touch with others. We need to encourage them and give them Biblical examples whom they can relate to and help them to keep things in perspective. We must remind them that they are fighting a really tough battle and are doing it in a courageous way (see Proverbs 24:16).

- *Example*—living like Jesus to the end, with dignity, self-control, courage and faith. Expect them to be the best example they can be. We need to help them find ways of completing goals. We must honor them and let them know how much we appreciate them and how they have inspired us all to be more like Jesus.

Discussing the Future

One of the larger spiritual issues with imminent death is the future, and one question that can arise with Christians helping someone living with illness is, "Are they spiritually ready to die?" This question can be the pink elephant sitting in the middle of the room that no one wants to talk about. We, the helpers, may or may not be the ones to address this issue with them, depending on their choice or their family's choice. However, it needs to be addressed at some point by someone. Talking about heaven, eternity or what will happen once we die can be very difficult because we may not be used to having discussions like these. But those living with illness may want to talk about it, and may not know how to bring it up— or may feel that they do not want to bother anyone with such a heavy topic. We can help by initiating the discussion and waiting to see if they pursue it. However, in order to be sensitive to the family's involvement and to their handling of the subject, we should ask the dying who else, if anyone, they are talking to about these things before we ourselves begin to speak. If it seems as if we are the ones who will have these discussions, we need to pray that God will give us wisdom (James 1:5) and that we will be able to speak from the Scriptures. We need to pray that God will direct our help and allow the dying a chance to discuss the deep issues of the heart that they possibly are facing.

Respecting Boundaries

> Carry each other's burdens, and in this way you will fulfill
> the law of Christ. (Galatians 6:2)

God expects us to help others carry their loads. This is love. Love is putting another person's needs before our own. We are commanded as Christians to love others; therefore, we need to love the dying with all our hearts. At the same time, we must be careful. In working with those living with illness, we cannot *love* them too much, but we can get too close. We can identify with their situations so much that we lose our objectivity, and as a result, become ineffective helpers. This can create difficulties for them such as communication problems, family disruptions and complications with the hospital staff and others. We must remember that we are helping, not crusading. It is helpful for us to ask for others' input on how we are doing in this area. This can help us guard against getting overwhelmed by their situations and doing the opposite of what we intend to do, which is help. If we truly want to "fulfill the law of Christ," we will seek proper boundaries that will allow us to love in the best way possible.

Faith, Hope and Love

Those who are dying need faith: faith to walk to the other side; faith to leave their relationships here behind; faith to believe that God will take care of what they did not finish; and faith to trust that God, their heavenly Father, will be with them all the way.

They also need hope: hope that does not take away their chances to find a cure, even if it's one in a million; hope that we will stay in there with their families; hope that in the end allows them to surrender and lay their burdens down.

Last, they need love: love that serves them with willing hearts and hands; love that imitates Jesus in seeking what is best for them; love that doesn't give in to fear; love that will not pull away, but will stay to the very end.

Non-Christians

There are some things that need to be especially considered when helping non-Christians. Listed below are some of these issues and recommended responses.

Conversion

Let us first consider the case of someone who is in immediate danger of dying and wants to get into a right relationship with God. We should get advice from those who have dealt with such situations if possible. We need to have an informed approach, rather that just rushing in. We must discern that *they* really want to learn about God and are interested in studying the Bible, and are not just being prompted by someone else. If they are in a hospital setting, there are hospital rules and doctors' directives that must be worked with and respected. Also understand that the time and energy available to them may be limited. They may be on medications and have specific regimens to follow which can compromise their ability to think, understand and process. This may limit their availability to study the Bible or talk. We need to have someone outside the situation help us to evaluate how things are going on a consistent basis. This enables us to keep helping with the situation without losing our objectivity. We must be urgent for people, but wise.

When studying the Bible with a person in these circumstances, focus on the basics: what is his view of God and does he want to have a relationship with him. Keep things simple and short. Do not spend large amounts of time looking at many scriptures when one will do. If time is limited, you cannot afford to have eight two-hour lessons only to arrive at the end of a detailed, systematic study series and have the person overtaken by his illness to the point he is unable to respond. Remember to focus on the person and his needs—not on teaching a great lesson or on the surroundings or even on the disease. Make eye contact, ask questions that get at the heart of the matter, listen to responses and do your best at making sure the person understands what you are talking about. Be sensitive. The disease and the shortened life span may have conspired to make this an emotionally charged time. Studying about God and the true meaning of life can bring about emotional upheaval even in the best of circumstances, so respect the person's wishes to slow down or stop if it becomes too much to handle emotionally. If he reaches a decision to be baptized, be aware that the baptism can present some logistic difficulties, but can be done even in a hospital setting. In all of this use good judgment; have at least one other person involved; get outside advice; and pray that God gives you time, wisdom and love to see it through.

Spiritual Talk

We may have the chance to bring up spiritual issues with non-Christians. Some may be interested, but others may not be. Though they are facing death, they still may not be open to God. We can never force the discussion if they are not willing, and yet, we should not pull away from them if they reject our offer. We need to remain their friends, and love and support them as best we can.

However, if someone is open to the discussion, we should pursue it at a time when we can talk without interference if possible. We must be wise about the discussion. Some may be open to exploring the subject, but not ready to open the Bible and deal with salvation. We need to pray that God will give them time and give us wisdom to communicate the truth effectively and quickly.

Respect

With non-Christians we must be more sensitive to the family dynamic. Family members may have different spiritual convictions and may view us as intruders on their faith. We need to be patient and loving; God can open doors, but there also may be limits to what we can do for the dying due to their current circumstance.

Be Faithful

There will be people who become Christians near the end of their lives. Crisis sobers all of us, and there will be those who earnestly repent and seek God in the face of death. We may be used by God to study the Bible with them and help them become Christians. Even so, we need to be humble and remember that it is God who has been at work for some time, getting them ready to respond to him.

Helping is like riding a bike alongside a friend. You cannot ride it for him, but you can assist, serve, inspire, love, cheer on and ride with your friend right to the end. Be prepared as best you can not only to help the dying, but to be personally changed by the great opportunity and blessing of riding next to some of life's greatest heroes.

Helping People with AIDS

If you are helping someone dying of AIDS, keep the following principles in mind.

- *Understand*—AIDS brings many challenges to the table. It is wise and helpful to do some reading or talk to someone who deals with AIDS patients regularly.

- *Search your own heart*—knowing where you stand spiritually in dealing with AIDS will help you be a better helper. You need to be honest and get help and advice about any beliefs or struggles you have with AIDS or its social implications.

- *Encourage adherence*—most AIDS patients have difficulty sticking with the drug regimens that are set up for them. If followed, they can provide relief and remission. There is no cure for AIDS yet, but with further development in drug treatments, there are now ways of slowing the virus down and providing a longer life span. This can in many cases only be achieved if the person is willing to be consistent with his medication regimen. One of the reasons that adherence is a challenge is due to the multiple side effects of the medications and the mental challenge of not seeing any use in fighting the virus continually.

- *Never take away hope*—hope may change over time. Be sensitive and informed about what hope there is for those who have AIDS and where they are in the progression of the illness.

- *Recognize the losses*—do your best to understand the multiple losses those with AIDS must deal with: health, validation from society, employment ability, free time, mobility, privacy, personality, dreams, future, etc. Those who have close associations with other AIDS patients can experience numerous losses in short periods of time due to the nature of the disease.

• *Allow them to grieve*—they will need to grieve all of the losses listed above. Helpers must give them "permission" to grieve when they are ready.

• *Assist them*—a multitude of situations will come up that he will need help with. Many of these will occur due to the fact that they cannot physically take care of themselves anymore. You may need a group of people who can act as a support, so that no one person ends up with the complete responsibility of providing the care.

• *Be with them*—having someone around who cares makes a tremendous difference. Do your best to make them feel comfortable both emotionally and physically.

• *Be prepared*—in many cases AIDS includes dementia and other neurological problems. You may actually lose someone long before you lose their body. It is the nature of the disease and can be most difficult to observe. Do your best to educate yourself and prepare for the battles that come while helping someone living with AIDS.

9
Helping the Caregiver

Blessed are the merciful for they will be shown
mercy.

Matthew 5:7

The following is a sample of the hard reality and the inde-
scribable pain that families go through when a loved one
is dying. It is from a mother whose son has terminal cerebral
palsy.

> If I were interested in improving this situation, and
> not just mad about the whole thing, I would offer
> some alternatives.... Because it's not just Gabriel's
> turn—it's my turn, too. I was crushed and over-
> whelmed when he had to take three different med-
> icines every day. It's now ten medicines, and I am
> still crushed. I was crushed when I had to do his IV
> infusions (the sterile water, the little alcohol pads).
> I'm crushed every time I feed him through his feed-
> ing tube (the enormous syringe, the sweet, clotted
> smell). He goes to sleep if you rock him and sing to
> him, but it's hard to sing when you are so crushed.
> If I am brave and think very hard about what we're
> doing and where we're going, I realize that I've been
> hoping the nurse and the social worker would take
> over for me. I've been hoping this would start being
> somebody else's life. But it's not somebody else's,
> it's mine: my boy, my pain, and my job, finally, to

hold my son's hand, stroke his hair, and be with him till he dies. But I'm not brave, I'm small and frightened, here at the edge of this darkness. Take this cup away from me. Take it away and give me back that sweet-smelling baby you promised.[1]

    This chapter is about how to help caregivers. The term caregiver has different meanings to different people. It will be used here in a general way to describe anyone who gives consistent help or assistance directly to those living with terminal illness or to those assisting those people. Usually a family member, relative or friend plays this role. This chapter will attempt to make you aware of the impact that serious illness has on the family, household and surrounding relationships, and provide suggestions for help that you might give to those involved. It should be underscored that this short treatment does not, and could not, touch on the many different situations that are brought about by dying, nor does it go into the depths of caregiving required for each. Just as many of you who have experience with caregiving can testify, this is a complex and challenging part of life to deal with, especially when it extends over a long period of time. Hopefully this chapter will foster some thinking about additional ways to serve the caregiver. There are numerous books available if you are interested in learning more about caregiving and caregivers. Some can be found in the reference section at the back of this book.

Practical Help

Recognizing Anticipatory Mourning

Families and others who care for those who are dying will in some way experience anticipatory mourning. This is the grief and mourning that the family begins to experience before the actual death as they experience all levels of loss: past, present and future. It begins when the process of dying starts and lasts until the actual death. The following example illustrates this:

> When a husband is dying, a wife may realize that she has already lost the help that he used to give her around the house (a past lost), that she is currently losing the vigorous ways in which he used to express his love for her (a present or ongoing loss), and that she will soon lose the comfort of his presence and their hope for a shared retirement (an expected or anticipated loss).[2]

An awareness of anticipatory mourning should help the family and caregivers to understand what they will be going through ahead of time and provide them the opportunity to prepare and cope in healthier ways. The goal is to give both those living with illness and the caregivers the best end-of-life experience possible.

Respite

Those living with a terminal illness often require around-the-clock care. Many times this is not covered under insurance plans and must be provided by family and friends. No one can supply continuous care without time off to regroup and recover. The stress and strain that caregivers are under can be tremendous. We can help by providing them with breaks, days off and times of refreshment and replenishment. Also, we can make sure that caregivers are getting spiritual respite by helping them find time off to be with God in prayer and in his word. They may even want someone to be with them at times to just sit and talk about God. If it is possible, we should be this kind of friend. The more a caregiver can stay connected with God, the better they will do in carrying out the duties of their role.

The Home Front

The wife of a close friend of mine who died of cancer told me the following suggestion for help with the home front: "If possible, caregivers should get a coordinator." They need to find someone they can communicate through and who can help coordinate things for the family. Unexpected events, hospital stays and emergencies require help in many ways. Having someone who can work with the caregiver makes situations more bearable. The coordinator may then feel free to pull other people into the helping role as she sees needs arising. Also, the coordinator can help with the following situations:

- *Laundry*—others can do the laundry. The coordinator can show the helpers how the caregiver wants it done and when it is needed.

- *Meals*—having meals put together can save caregivers time and energy. The coordinator can communicate the likes, dislikes, allergies or special diets of the caregiver, and can ask people to use disposable containers to save the time of washing and returning dishes. She can also coordinate others to prepare food supplied by the caregiver since some want to serve but cannot always bear the expense.

- *Children*—help is always appreciated with baby-sitting, sleepovers, transportation to games and events, school projects, mentoring, encouragement at activities, and simple attention. This keeps routines as normal as they can be for caregivers and their families.

- *Cleaning and errands*—the caregiver needs to communicate to the coordinator about the best times for cleaning so as to avoid disrupting the home front. Also, the coordinator can make sure that odors or chemicals from cleaning supplies do not bother those living with illness, who may be more sensitive to smell.

- *Finances*—if the caregiver is not good at paperwork, the coordinator can help with bills or find someone early on who can. Insurance claims and medical bills alone can be enough to consume any one person— and if they are not handled properly, unnecessary additional expenses could be incurred.

- *Transportation*—the caregiver might need help with rides to hospitals, doctors' offices or pharmacies— especially if the caregiver is working a full-time job.

A Safe Place

Grief and mourning and living daily with those who are dying bring out the worst in many caregivers. The caregiver must have a place, system, time or haven in which to talk, cry, share, express, vent and unload the business of the day without fear of immediate overreaction, confrontation or judgment. This safe place will encourage continual openness and will provide the basis for diffusing problems and negative emotions that, left unchecked, can damage and even destroy the relationships of caregivers with each other.

Friends of caregivers may be called upon to help set up times to mediate when difficulties among families arise and to check on the caregivers from time to time to see if things are continuing to go okay. Experience has shown that it is only a matter of time before a group of caregivers need help as they minister to a dying person. When giving one-on-one advice to a caregiver, helpers must remember to keep the whole group of caregivers in mind. There is great temptation to be swayed to one person's side. This bias could render future attempts to help ineffective.

Last, keep in mind that caregivers and families are diverse. No easy, one-size-fits-all piece of advice or counsel will eliminate the hard work of building a safe place in which a family may receive the support it needs.

Advocacy

Caregivers and families often need someone else to speak up for them and their needs. This person may be the coordinator discussed above or someone else who can ask for help, find resources, update others and fulfill various other needs.

Education

Do not assume that caregivers totally understand the situation they are in. Helpers can serve them by providing perspective and education regarding death and dying (books, resources, other people who have been through a similar experience and the like). However, we need to be sure that we know what we are talking about before advising others. Near the end the caregiver or family will need to know about what to expect at the actual time of death. They may need to seek out resources such as hospice, which can inform them and prepare them for the coming challenges.

Connections

It is important that caregivers stay connected to other professional resources such as health-care providers, physicians and insurance companies. This may be a new role that they are adjusting to, and they may need encouragement to ask for help, and also to maintain a consistent, positive and right attitude toward these professionals who are also involved in the care of their loved one. For instance, books like *The Rights of the Dying* by David Kessler give suggestions about how caregivers can learn to work with physicians and get the help and answers they need.[3]

Relationships

Caregivers may require help in managing other outside relationships of those who are ill. Sometimes circumstances change quickly, and caregivers need to ask visitors to be flexible, or they may need to reduce the number of visitors altogether. This can be difficult emotionally, but as those living with illness decline, they may prefer to save their available energy to focus on a narrowing circle of relationships. Helpers may need to support caregivers and reassure them that they are doing the right thing in this situation.

After Death

The actual moment of death can be a very challenging one to experience. Many forget about the fact that the caregiver, after the death, returns to a home that is no longer occupied by a father, mother or child that only hours before was at the center of the life of the family. A room or a bed will be empty and the regimen, voices, routine and presence of the deceased will all be gone. We can help by thinking ahead for the caregiver. If their family member or friend died in a hospital, we may offer to return home with them from the hospital and straighten up or sleep over. We may need to make sure they get rest after the long ordeal of death. They may need our help cleaning the next day as they begin to make plans for the memorial service. Or we may simply need to call them and tell them we love them and will come by the next day to help.

Spiritual Help

Prayer

Prayer is invaluable in lifting, sustaining, comforting and healing caregivers. Helpers can share with them that they and others are praying for them (see Philippians 4:6 and James 5:15). When we don't know what to pray specifically, we can just ask God to hold the dying and the caregivers close to his heart.

Respect

Caregivers need our respect (1 Peter 2:17). They might have a different spiritual outlook than we do. They might not think things through logically. They might not be as decisive as we would like them to be. It doesn't matter; if we want to help we must respect them and their decisions. This means respecting them even if their decisions might be different from those we would make. It means respecting them even if they make mistakes. However, in the end they should know we recognize that they, not us, are the ones who have to live with the ill and will have to make the difficult decisions. They need to know that over the long haul we will respect them, support them and continue to give them assistance.

Validation

At times we will need to say, "What you are going through is normal for your situation." For instance, when caregivers are feeling that people don't understand the challenges they are facing daily, your acknowledging their frustration is very important to them. It tells them that what they are experiencing is valid to someone else. They need us to accept their emotions for what they are. It does not mean that their response to or expression of those emotions will always be correct, but we must validate what they are legitimately feeling. We cannot continually theorize about what we think they should be feeling or accept only our perception of what is going on with their situation because this eventually will alienate caregivers and cause them to disregard our opinions on spiritual and other more important matters.

Resolution

The need to work through unfinished business applies to the caregiver or family of a dying person no less than it does to the one who is dying. We can encourage caregivers or family members to deal with any unresolved issues (forgiveness, attitudes, conflicts, abuse and more) with them or the rest of the family. They may need our presence to accomplish this. However, this is something *they* must do or not do. We cannot resolve their business for them or make them feel that they must do it. We can urge them to do it, suggest ways to accomplish it, and can even mediate for them, but in the end, we need to respect their choice to deal with it or not.

Perseverance

We need to stick with them (see Hebrews 12:1 and 2 Peter1:6). This can be a long race and many will drop out early. This can be especially true after the death. During these times, anything can happen. People can plummet spiritually and otherwise. If they retreat, we cannot give up on them. They need to know that no matter what, even if they walk away from God, we care about them and will be there for them. We should not force our agenda on the caregiver, but give them space to grow and give God room to work.

The Final Days

The fact is that in America most people will spend their final days in a hospital. Only a small percentage will die in their homes. More will be said about this in chapter 12, but we should remember that hospitals can be a challenging place for the end of life, due to the sterile environment, the machines and equipment, and the cramped, impersonal rooms and waiting rooms. We can help by being there, making people as comfortable as we can, respecting hospital rules (especially noise, visiting hours and cell phone use), limiting the number of phone calls and visitors, helping with errands, or just bringing a card or flower. We need to be careful not to be intrusive as helpers. Although those who are dying may be our friends, they are the family's father, mother, brother or child. We need to remember that it is a great privilege and honor to be included by the family in saying good-bye to the dying.

Be aware of the great challenges and needs faced by care-givers as they love and serve the dying. In all probability you will assume the same role at some point in your life. Thinking about how you would want to be treated can guide you as you seek to help others who face such challenges now. Although at times difficult, caring for the caregivers can bring lasting and meaningful experiences that will be felt long after their loved ones have died.

When our dad was in the final stages of Alzheimer's disease, my sister and I made the difficult decision to request that no feeding tube be placed in him when he was no longer able to eat. At that point we wanted the nurses to hydrate him and make him as comfortable as possible. We were with him when his body finally gave in to the disease. He mercifully breathed his last. The end was bittersweet. We had actually lost our dad months earlier. His body had just stayed around, reminding us of who he was and how much we loved him. We said our final good-byes to this gentle, loving man who had taught us to love God and other people, and to have integrity in every situation. He was so much bigger than the shriveled little body he lived in. He was a hero. He was our dad.

—Sheila

10
Complicated Grief and Mourning

I received an e-mail from Bill a number of years ago. For a long time his mother had lived with a debilitating heart condition. She had been in and out of the hospital numerous times throughout the years, each time a critical situation that worsened her condition. In the end she developed complications and lapsed into a coma.

After the hospital staff had expended every measure of effort, the family was approached by one of the doctors to discuss taking her off life support. He stated that she would continue to experience complications that would eventually kill her, that she showed no brain functioning at the present time and that she would not, in their opinion, regain any such functioning. The doctor asked them to think it over, but indicated that they ought to remove life support and let her die peacefully.

For the rest of the family it was clear that this was the right decision. They understood that her brain had ceased to function and her life was technically over; it was time to recognize this and let her go quietly. For Bill it was different. He had become a Christian a short time before, and at this hour the thought that tore at his heart the most was not that he was losing his mother, but that he never had talked to her about having a relationship with God. Now he was faced with giving his consent to a decision that would end her life, leaving him no chance of ever talking with her again.

As the family gathered around, her life support was removed. They waited, not knowing how long she would actually live without it. As her breathing became labored, Bill stood near her bed, gazing at her. All of a sudden, she opened her eyes, looked straight at him, said "I love you" and then closed her eyes. She died an hour later.

Bill came to believe that he had contributed to the death of his mother. He was haunted by the thought that she could have lived, that the doctors were wrong, that he would have had the opportunity to talk to her about God. But her life was over, and he could not shake being angry at himself, thinking that God was also angry with him. He did not know how to deal with this. I encouraged him to get some professional help to deal with his grief and to seek spiritual help from those in the church he attended. I offered whatever aid, encouragement or phone calls I could give him—and then Bill disappeared. I am not sure what happened to him. I lost contact with him, and can only hope that he received the help and support he needed to deal with this difficult loss.

Difficult deaths, such as the one discussed above, and their contributing factors have the potential of complicating the mourning process by interfering with and interrupting grief. Generally the phrase used to describe this is "complicated grief and mourning."

Knowing ahead of time the types of deaths that are especially difficult for people to work through can help us to consider how the loss may affect them and the potential challenges they may face in mourning. If the bereaved do not seem to be working well through mourning or they seem to be experiencing a greater and greater degree of dysfunction, then it is important to consider that there may be something "complicating" their mourning that may demand more focused help.

I have two warnings I would ask you to heed before going forward. First, this chapter is not intended to make you a psychiatrist or therapist overnight by providing you with a simple and easy litmus test for determining if a person is experiencing complicated mourning. What this information is intended to do is to make you more aware of extenuating circumstances surrounding a death and the difficult issues they bring to grief and mourning. Second, it is important that you do not rush to judgment about how a person is doing too soon after a death—unless you have reason to believe his or her (or others') life or health could be in danger. If you are concerned about how the bereaved is doing, then talk to him and encourage him to seek professional help if necessary.

Complicated Deaths

The following deaths are ones in which circumstances can lead to complicated grief and mourning. First we will look some general factors that can complicate death and mourning. Then we will look at some specific types of death that also can bring complications to grief and mourning.

Sudden and unanticipated deaths can complicate mourning especially if they involve trauma, violence, mutilation or accident. For instance, a bad car accident can present horrifying images of the death as well as a whole different level of circumstances to deal with such as police reports, investigations, jury trial, etc.

Deaths that occur after a long illness can create potential problems for the bereaved. One such problem could be that family life could have been put on hold for years due to the family member's illness. Once the person is gone, the family discovers that their lives have not developed or matured during the time of the disease and that numerous needs went unmet during that period of time.

Deaths that are not supported by our society (i.e., suicide, AIDS) may result in the griever not being recognized and supported. Our society is making progress in this area, but many families and friends still feel the difficulty of openly and comfortably mourning a death of this type.

Death in which the relationship was characterized by anger, ambivalence or extreme dependence can signal potential problems. If the bereaved person was abused by a father who is now dead, mourning can be especially difficult and confusing. The complicating dilemma is whether the bereaved should feel sad about the loss of his father or happy that now the perpetrator will not be around to cause more pain.

Complications can also occur when the bereaved feel a lack of support. If the bereaved person senses this lack of support it may inhibit his proceeding down a path of mourning that could appear frightening or impossible to live through.

Also, prior medical or mental conditions can set the bereaved up for difficulty with death. Someone who experiences depression may have a greater degree of trouble with a death than others.

Finally, a prior loss that has not been mourned or worked through can complicate situations surrounding a new loss. A new loss may not be mourned because the prior loss brings unfinished business to the table to be dealt with as well.

Perinatal

"Perinatal death refers to the death of infants after the twentieth week of gestation and through at least the first month after birth."[1] Perinatal deaths such as miscarriage, still-birth and neonatal death have a number of common challenges, which are listed here. Certain of these issues will be more pertinent than others depending upon the type of death.[2]

- The pregnancy was planned and desired.
- A long time or infertility treatments were needed to get pregnant (heightening fear that future pregnancy might not occur).
- History of elective abortions and residual guilt (miscarriage seen as punishment).
- No warning signs, little time to prepare.
- Loss occurring late in pregnancy.
- History of losses (multiple miscarriages, current loss triggers earlier grief).
- Strain between partners.
- History of poor coping, especially depression.
- Death is not acknowledged by family or friends.

Miscarriage

"Miscarriage or spontaneous abortion is defined as an unintended termination of pregnancy before the twentieth week of gestation."[3] Some of the challenges with miscarriage are as follows:

- *It is not recognized as a loss.* Typically, miscarriage is not recognized as a loss by many people, but it genuinely is. To the woman who is pregnant, a baby is a baby although he is only weeks old. Even during a short time, hopes, dreams and expectations have already begun to form, but because others do not know the baby, the grief of miscarriage is often underestimated.

- *Couples need to be able to grieve.* Couples who have a miscarriage need to be allowed to grieve. The extent of this grief will be determined by the factors listed above and the extent of the relationship already created by the couple with the baby.

Some of the ways in which mourning the loss can be facilitated are seeing signs of the death (the fetus), naming the fetus, having a memorial service and writing a letter or poem which captures the thoughts and feelings that were created during the time of pregnancy. Allowing the couple to share their story assists them in developing a narrative that will serve them in validating, remembering and working their way through the loss.

Stillbirth

Some of the unique challenges associated with stillbirths are as follows:

- *Carried longer*—different from miscarriage, stillbirth babies are carried in utero longer, thus creating a greater attachment to the baby.

- *Returning home*—it is extremely difficult to come home from a hospital with no baby to show for all the changes and work that the parents went through during those months.

- *Limited support*—at a time when support is needed, grief is shared with a limited number of people since the baby was not known to many.

- *Prior preparations*—a home prepared for the arrival of a new baby can hold many poignant and painful reminders.

- *Guilt*—stillbirth can generate guilt in many ways, such as suspicions of having harmed the baby, possible lack of attention to the woman's health, some other cause of body failure, and more.

- *Children*—siblings must be given information sensitively and correctly and may need to be talked with about any ambivalent feelings they had toward the new brother or sister.

- *Physical changes*—the woman's body is still acting as if a baby had arrived.

- *Father's grief*—fathers may be overlooked in the grieving process.

Couples who experience a stillbirth may be helped in their grieving by looking at and holding the dead baby. If possible, they should take part in the certification of the stillbirth. Parents need to be able to name the baby and keep any tangible reminders, such as a nametag, pictures or clothing to help them remember the short time they had with their child. Also, the couple should be given the choice to hold a memorial or funeral service for the baby, which can serve to validate their experience and memories and bring some closure to the death. After the death make sure to ask the parents if there are any lingering issues concerning pre-death medical treatment or decisions. Unresolved issues can lead to future complications with relationships and future pregnancies. It would be wise for couples to seek advice when the time comes for considering another pregnancy so that any unresolved issues of mourning can be talked through before proceeding.

Neonatal

Neonatal death is the death of a newborn infant, whether premature or full term, within the first twenty-eight days. The additional challenges neonatal deaths bring include

- *Treatment dilemmas*—the question of whether further medical intervention during the first twenty-eight days will bring the desired outcome of a healthy life. Also, the spiritual and psychological challenge parents face when deciding whether or not to end treatment.

- *The issue of pain*—parents are always concerned about whether the baby is suffering or not.

- *Everyday life*—a baby in intensive care can stop family life in its tracks. It can be a challenge to spend continual time at the hospital waiting to see what will happen. Some employers may not be supportive of this type of extended leave, which can add to the pressure felt by the couple.

- *Finances*—the cost of neonatal care can be extremely expensive.

For some specific suggestions to facilitate mourning, refer to the preceding section on stillbirth.

SIDS

Sudden Infant Death Syndrome (SIDS) is the death of a child less than one year of age. The cause of SIDS is still unknown. The specific difficulties that SIDS brings are

- *Death without warning*—SIDS strikes unexpectedly.

- *No definite cause*—SIDS causes suspicion to be placed on the parents. This in turn can cause the parents to feel intense guilt and blame. It also launches a relentless search for meaning, beginning with the cause of the death.

- *Legal issues*—SIDS deaths are open to investigation that can lead to interrogation and sometimes incarceration. This type of pressure is extremely difficult to bear in the midst of grief.

- *Individual reactions*—couples have a very tough time dealing with each other's grieving over the death of a child. This is a common problem and often necessitates getting help from outside the marriage to work through mourning together.

Some additional things that can help parents work through a SIDS death are

- *Hospital intervention*—hopefully the hospital will provide support in a SIDS death if the child was brought to a medical facility. This support can be in the form of giving the parents the option of spending time with the dead child, holding or dressing the child, taking pictures, etc.

- *Autopsy permission*—parents can be sensitively encouraged to accept a postmortem examination (autopsy). This can give them the chance to learn about any facts regarding the cause of death. It provides a sense of reality to the death as well. Having the exam can also help in settling the insurance issues that will ensue after a SIDS death.

- *Information*—parents need to be given information on grief, SIDS, future pregnancy and support groups. These can go a long way in describing the challenges they face and providing them with resources to help them through this time.

Abortion

Those who have had or have been involved with elective abortions should be encouraged to review their circumstances and evaluate whether or not they mourned the loss of their baby. Even though Christians can come to terms with past abortions and experience God's forgiveness, they may not have mourned the loss of the baby. This lack of mourning can be a set up for difficulty later in life—especially for dealing with future losses. Any man who has encouraged or participated in a decision for an abortion would do well to ask himself if he mourned the loss. It is easy to forget that both the man and the woman have suffered a loss and that both will be affected by it.

Death of a Child

The death of a child is an extremely challenging death to deal with. Mourning the loss of a child is a long, painful journey. As Dennis Klass put it,

> When a child dies, the parent experiences an irreparable loss, because the child is an extension of

the parent's self. Parental bereavement is a permanent condition. Bereaved parents do adjust in the sense that they learn to invest themselves in other tasks and other relationships. Still, somewhere inside themselves, they report there is a sense of loss that cannot be healed.[4]

Therese Rando writes,

Parents who lose a child are multiply victimized. We are victimized by the realistic loss of the child we love, we are victimized by the loss of the dreams and hopes we had invested in that child, and we are victimized by the loss of our own self-esteem. Not unlike the survivors of the concentration camps, we cannot comprehend why we did not die instead.[5]

Being the Parent

Losing a child can challenge us to the core about our ability to be a parent. It causes us to question whether we are capable of caring, loving, protecting and fulfilling all the responsibilities of having a child. It is good to have others help us deal with this type of harsh self-analysis; we need people who can validate our abilities as parents.

Another challenge of losing a child is that we lose a part of ourselves as well. Think for a moment about all that you, as a son or daughter, represent to your parent(s), such as being the giver, the great athlete, the family storyteller and more. Then think about what would be lost from their lives if you died. When a child dies, the relationship, hopes, happiness, dreams, future and all that we would have gained and experienced through our children are all swept away in death. We lose that significant part of us that only comes by being a parent. Many say that this particular loss cannot be repaired because a part of us has been lost forever. Therefore, if we are helping bereaved parents, it is good to remember and support them through the added losses that they feel. It is also important to realize that though the hurt will always be there, parents report that they are able to still have joy in life as they continue on their journey.

'It's Not Supposed to Work This Way'

Most people feel that a child should never die before a parent, especially in an era when everything is potentially curable and we have the technology to keep people alive to a ripe old age. But unfortunately it still happens. This commonly held view of life makes it difficult to comprehend, accept and work through the death of a child. Also, age is not a determinant. Whether the child is four or forty, it never feels right to lose a child.

Responses of Others

When we lose a child, people can respond in insensitive ways. Some may avoid us altogether because the death makes them aware that it could also happen to them. In addition, the bereaved are often told, "At least you have other children," thinking that this is somehow going to console them. Others may mistakenly reason that since it is "just a child," your grief should not last as long as it would for the death of an adult whom you have been with for years. Be prepared—this type of thinking can lead to many insensitive comments.

Understanding Each Other

Grieving and mourning the death of a child can cause extreme stress on the marriage relationship. To begin with, both parents will respond differently to the death. It can be said that men and women grieve differently, but it may be more exact to say that there are "instrumental" grievers and "intuitive" grievers.[6]

Instrumental grievers (which we might generally consider to be men) respond to grief by doing, fixing, writing, solving or working. They tend to have some way other than talking to work through or express their grief. Intuitive grievers (generally women) are helped much more in their grief by talking or getting things out in the open. They may come to learn or understand more by the exchanging of information, stories or emotion. This may explain why there can be difficulty with both husband and wife understanding the other's response to loss. While the wife wants the husband to open up and talk about it, the man may want her to stop bringing it up and leave him alone so he can deal with it. The only way he may see to cope is to get out of the situation and turn his attention to something that lets him "work out his grief" such as mowing the yard or washing the car. She on the other hand may feel the need for constant dialogue, remembering and tears.

This difference in coping and expression can be extremely frustrating to both husband and wife, and it tempts them to believe that the "other person" is wrong in how he or she is handling grief. Intervention may be required to help one or both see and respect the other's journey through mourning, which ultimately can draw them together as they live through the loss, rather than separating them.

Why?

Seeking an answer to the question "Why?" may be the toughest challenge a parent faces. The death of a child may call into question God's parenting ability, just as it does our own. Trying to make spiritual sense or meaning out of the death of a child is a long, frustrating process that brings out the good and bad in us. It is normal for parents to raise spiritual questions and look for spiritual answers at a time when answers may not make sense. Furthermore, people can be quick to give right answers at the wrong time and further hurt the bereaved. Sometimes the question of "Why?" that the bereaved asks someone is more of a rhetorical question, requiring no immediate answer. (More on this subject can be found in chapters 3 and 4.)

Guilt

Many parents can suffer "survivor's guilt." Some parents feel so guilty about outliving a child that it can cause thoughts of wanting to join the deceased child in death. Although these thoughts are very normal, they should not be ignored. Also, others may experience guilt if they think that the death was preventable or that they were part of causing it. This type of guilt must be investigated and worked through or it too will complicate mourning. (This is addressed some in chapter 2.)

Suicide

Experience shows that suicide survivors are commonly affected by a number of challenging issues.

- *Greater guilt*—survivors may blame themselves for not having seen it coming, for not having prevented it or for not being able to explain why it happened.

Others may blame the bereaved and tend to avoid him or her.

- *Less social support*—there may be less social support for the bereaved since suicide is often dealt with in a quiet, discreet way due to the nature of the death and the social stigma attached to it. People often pull back and do not talk to the bereaved, consequently shrinking the circle of help and support that is needed.

- *A greater need to know why the death occurred*—most often with suicide, there are no answers to explain the death. The bereaved must live with many unanswered questions. It has been said by someone that the skeletons of the deceased move from his closet to the closet of the bereaved.

Additional reactions to suicide may include a continual search for a motive, denial that the death occurred, feelings of being rejected by the deceased, questions concerning the person's spiritual destiny, a desire to conceal the death and even a fear that suicide might be hereditary. All of these can lead to a protracted and intense period of grief and mourning. (See chapters 5 and 6 for more help regarding this subject.)

AIDS

The mourning of deaths as a result of AIDS is, without a doubt, complicated. Part of the complication is due to the fact that grievers will experience grief and mourning long before the actual death of a loved one. They may live through multiple losses of long-time friends and others they have come to know as a result of their disease. They may also experience mourning more acutely due to AIDS being a death that society does not easily recognize and support. As a result they may

fear grieving publicly due to the stigma or feel relatively isolated in obtaining support. We must do a better job of understanding these situations because current statistics predict
that we will continue to encounter an increasing number of
AIDS deaths worldwide.

There are a number of complicating factors associated
with those living with AIDS/HIV.[7] One is the ongoing reality of
losing numerous relationships, both previous and new, with
those who also have AIDS/HIV. This loss of relationships
brings a loss of resources and support. There can be a certain
level of ongoing fear in starting new relationships with
AIDS/HIV affected people due to the fact that you stand to
lose them at some point in the future. The idea of numerous
deaths to grieve while battling your own situation can seem
like too much to deal with. Also, friends and family who do
not have AIDS/HIV can be fearful of being around someone
who does, and this fear can cause them to pull away and not
be a support to the affected person. Additional pain can be
realized as some even face instances of discrimination.
Finally, practical as well as mental complications can be felt
when health-care professionals' response to treatment for
people living with AIDS can be insufficient due to the lack of
workers willing to work with AIDS/HIV patients.

For more help regarding living with AIDS or helping those
living with AIDS, see chapters 7 and 8 respectively.

In this chapter I have attempted to shed some light on certain types of complicated grief and mourning. This does not
constitute an exhaustive review of each type of death nor the

specifics that come with that death. It is incumbent upon you to get the necessary help and information about the kind of death that you happen to be confronted by or are helping with. Hopefully this has made you more aware of the difficulties different deaths bring and has given you some understanding and guidance in meeting the complicated needs of the dying and bereaved.

Spiritual Notes

The "Spiritual Notes" at the end of chapters 2 and 3 apply to the subject of complicated mourning as well. But as we have seen, difficult deaths can bring complications to the mourning process, and we may find that they also produce more spiritual challenges. Knowing this may call for increased attention to the spiritual health of the bereaved.

Trust

Death in general causes us to feel vulnerable in our world. Difficult deaths can increase this feeling of vulnerability. Spiritually we may wrestle with trust in God because we feel that he did not protect the deceased or that his power failed to stop the death. We may even feel that we are in some way being punished by the death of our loved one. However, we need to maintain our trust in God. We must not buy into the lies that Satan tells us: that God is not powerful enough or does not care or is out to get us. God's power and care are not dependent on receiving explanations; Job learned this lesson firsthand. God knew that in the end Job's belief and trust would prevail. God commends Job's trust when he said to his friends,

"I am angry with you [Eliphaz the Temanite] and your
friends, because you have not spoken of me what is right,
as my servant Job has." (Job 42:7)

Truth

One of the difficult things about a complicated death is that
we want to know the truth, but the truth may never be known.
Accidental death is often devoid of explanation. Even the
experts may only give us their opinions. Jesus said that the
"truth will set you free," and when there is no truth, it can be
more difficult to find meaning in a death. We may need to
decide at some point how we are going to spiritually respond to
the lack of information. We may decide that there are spiritual
truths that we need to re-embrace, such as what God spoke to
Joshua: "I will never leave you nor forsake you" (Joshua 1:5).
God is still there even if all the answers are not, and he hopes
that we will hang on rather than let go. Also, there are certain
basic truths that we may need to reconsider, such as suffering
is hard but is a part of life (John 16:33); our physical bodies will
fail in time (2 Corinthians 5:1–5); the world is filled with risk and
danger (Acts 14:19); and sickness will occur (2 Kings 20:1). All
too often we leave these truths out of the picture when searching for meaning in complicated deaths.

Faith

In Romans 4:19–22 Paul writes that Abraham "faced the
fact" about his body being too old to reproduce. Nevertheless
he continued to hold on to his faith in the promise of God—he
"was strengthened in his faith and gave glory to God, being
fully persuaded that God had power to do what he had promised" (Romans 4:20–21).

Complicated death can bring intense grief because of its sudden, unpredictable and traumatic nature. We may need some lessons from people like Abraham, who was determined not to become a victim of his circumstances. First, he looked at the scanty facts that were available to him about their infertility and probably did not have many answers. I'm sure over the years of trying to have a child after God had given him the promise, the lack of facts produced many questions and emotions, but "he did not waver" in his faith (Romans 4:20). He did not let the facts—or lack of them—overwhelm his faith in the promises of God.

Intrusive thoughts, dreams, assumptions and our imagination will be challenging to deal with, but we need to get help to not let them overwhelm us to the point of throwing away God's truths. Abraham refused to let either the "unknowns" or the "knowns" of his situation turn him against God and into an angry, bitter man.

Second, the Bible says that upon facing his circumstances and determining to trust in God he "was strengthened in his faith" (Romans 4:20). I am convinced that if in mourning we continue to face the facts with faith and work through matters with God, we will get stronger spiritually, which will help us through our mourning journey. By letting God remain God, "giving him the glory," sticking with our convictions that he is all-powerful, and "being fully persuaded" even though our situation was allowed to happen, we will be strengthened (Romans 4:20–21).

I am not trying to minimize pain or to say this is easy, but it can be done. We must mourn our loss, but not let complicated deaths and the lack of understanding and meaning push us away from God and his truth. We need to take courage and

MOURNING JOURNEY

not let the "unbelievers" in this world persuade us to let go of our faith. They will simplistically claim that since our loss was so tragic, traumatic and beyond understanding that God's character and what he says are questionable and unreasonable. Jesus tells us the real truth when he says, "In this world you will have trouble. But take heart! I have overcome the world" (John 16:33).

My Story
The Loss of My Babies
Gloria Baird

As a young married couple still in college, our life was before us; our future was full of hope and dreams. One of those dreams became a reality a little earlier than we had expected when I learned that I was pregnant. We were thrilled with the news and loved sharing it with our families, especially since this would be the first grandchild for both sets of parents.

My pregnancy went very well, and I stayed busy with college and planning for the arrival of our baby. Much to our surprise I went into labor about seven weeks before the baby was due. Despite all attempts to stop my labor, our baby boy was born, weighing four pounds and ten ounces. It was soon evident that he had respiratory problems and needed special treatment.

After three days of struggling, he died. Somehow, in our youthful thinking, we had never imagined anything like this happening to us. A time that should have been one of the happiest moments in our life suddenly became overwhelmingly sorrowful. One of the biggest lessons we learned at that time was that we, too, were vulnerable—hard things could happen to us!

Facing people for the first time after our baby died was very challenging. Since I was in school at the time, my classmates were excited when I came back not pregnant, and immediately asked about our baby. It was awkward for them and me when I had to tell them that we had lost him. One of my close friends was pregnant at the same time, so my loss made it hard for us to communicate. I realized that I had to dig deep with God, not only for my own strength, but also to be able to talk with others and put them at ease around us. Not having experienced a loss or tragedy like this, we were amazed at the strength that God supplied at just the right time. Our faith in God helped us accept our loss, whether we understood it or not. We certainly asked "Why?" yet we did not demand the answer, knowing and trusting that God knew best.

Getting pregnant again about three months later helped us to look ahead rather than focus on our loss. Thankfully, our daughter Staci arrived safe and sound even though she came five weeks early.

Al and I wanted our children about two years apart, so we got pregnant again. I was very optimistic and felt that surely everything would go well this time. We had learned that we could experience hardship, and it seemed to me that we already had experienced our share. My doctor watched me closely during this pregnancy because of my history. Because I began dilating between my sixth and seventh month, he diagnosed my problem as an incompetent cervix. He sent me to the hospital immediately to have corrective surgery that same day. Shortly before I was to go into surgery I went into labor. Although efforts were again made to stop my labor, I soon delivered not one baby, but two—twin girls—each weighing a little over two pounds. They both lived about twenty-four hours and then we lost them, too.

This all happened so fast and unexpectedly—it was hard to believe that we were going through this again...and with twins! This time we knew from previous experience what some of our feelings and struggles would be, but we also knew how we had endured our other loss: with God's incredible strength and the love and support of our family and friends. I remember not so much what people said to us at those times, but people just being there with us. It seems that every need we had was met—from financial help for the burial and funeral (which was very needed since Al was still in graduate school) to food, flowers and even a gift certificate to a restaurant for a future date for Al and me. Obviously, that gift stands out to me even years later as I realize it gave us something to look forward to beyond our immediate loss.

After losing the twins, we realized that we do not determine our "share" of hardships. Life will hold some things that we may never understand. Our comfort was to know that God does understand and care about our heartaches and pain. With each loss heaven became dearer to us as we held on to God's eternal perspective. Certainly, having Staci, our toddler, at home made an incredible difference and helped us remember the blessing of life rather than focusing totally on our losses.

Another lesson I learned through the deaths of our babies was that it was my own choice how I responded to difficult situations. Generally, people are very supportive and helpful around the tragic event, but then life goes on very quickly for those not directly affected. If I had curled up in a corner, grieving for months, I would have found myself alone. I found that I had to be open and share with others when I felt sad, rather than expect them to be aware of my feelings and struggles.

Shortly after we lost our twins, I had corrective surgery to put a tie around my cervix so future births would require cesarean delivery. When I had healed from this surgery, I got pregnant again. After all we had experienced, I was aware of every ache or pain I felt, and had to fight anxious and fearful thoughts. Trusting God and continually remembering how he had strengthened us helped me to fight those fears. Having the corrective surgery and planning the date for the C-section made me feel more at peace. That peace was shaken when I went into labor a month early; it wasn't supposed to happen like that! I had an emergency C-section and delivered our daughter Kristi. We were so relieved and grateful that she was healthy and had no respiratory problems. It is amazing how the joy of a new baby helps to soothe the pain and fill some of the void from loss.

When Kristi was about two years old, Al and I decided we would try one more time to complete our family. As with all my pregnancies, I was very healthy during this one too. I stayed busy and active with our two little girls, but of course, still had to fight anxious feelings. To my dismay, I again had premature labor—this time five weeks before my due date, necessitating another emergency C-section. We were overjoyed at the safe arrival of our daughter Keri. It seemed that everything was fine—until she began to have breathing difficulty when she was two days old. Because of our history, the doctors decided she should be taken to a special hospital where she could get the necessary treatment. I remember this being one of my most intense struggles. I thought surely this could not be happening again. It was a time I wrestled with God's will, crying out in agony, telling God that I could not stand to lose another baby! Somehow I believe God helped me to remember how he brought us through the other times of loss, so that I could surrender, knowing that he would supply the strength to endure another loss if that happened again. Even in the midst of my pain, I was able to feel a peace and calm that could only come from God. Right after this we got the report that Keri improved on the ambulance ride to the hospital. The admitting doctors wondered why she was brought there! We are sure Keri is our "miracle" baby.

I often wonder what kind of people Al and I would be had we not experienced these challenges and losses. There are so many life lessons that God taught us through these experiences. Going through our own times of pain and disappointment has enabled us to feel with others with similar heartaches. Keeping a spiritual perspective not only strengthened us and others at the time of loss, but later helped us realize that because of our losses and the subsequent births of our three daughters, we can have six children for eternity—and that is what really counts!

11
Decisions We All Need to Make

Lynn, a friend of mine in her thirties, has cancer. During the last few years she has faced hundreds of decisions that she never thought about before. She was not prepared to make them so soon and so young. Her early decisions were immediate as she had to ask demanding questions: "Can we schedule you for surgery?" and "Can we start the treatment tomorrow?" But these were only the beginning. Every decision seemed to lead to other decisions: "Should I trust this doctor or get another opinion?" "If I get other opinions, will this doctor be hard to work with down the road?" "Where do I go to find accurate information about my particular type of cancer?" "Should I consider unconventional medical treatments?" "How much time do I have to shop around?"

Lynn did an admirable job handling the many choices that came her way. She learned how to get the information, explanations and answers she needed to make the best decisions possible. She learned to sit and wrestle with situations until she felt resolved about her course of action. She was respectful but not timid when it came to getting answers and understanding her health situation.

But medical decisions are not the only ones she has had to make. There were personal decisions: "Do I change my diet?" "What do I do about a will?" "How about end-of-life issues and funeral arrangements?" Family decisions surfaced such as "Should I ask if anyone in my family can take care of me if I am unable to do so?" Financial decisions had to be tackled, such as "How will I continue to pay my bills without being able to work?" These are not the kinds of decisions a young person would normally be wrestling with, but they had to be made all the same. As the days and weeks and months went by, Lynn's situation changed numerous times. With each change, she had to rethink earlier decisions she had made in light of her ever-changing circumstances.

Throughout her ordeals, Lynn faced spiritual decisions as well. These were perhaps the most challenging, and Lynn would say that she has done the best she could at making them. At times it is hard to know what the best decision is. A medical decision can seem to conflict with a spiritual one. "Do I choose not to have a particular surgery that might lengthen my life but make it miserable for me physically day to day?" or "Do I just allow the disease to run its course and do what I can while staying focused and spiritually alert?" "When do I decide to stop fighting the disease and use the time to do other meaningful things such as reconciliation, family preparation, recording my life's story or fulfilling a last experience?"

Lynn has often wrestled with these decisions, and yet perhaps the most difficult decision has been "What else needs to be done spiritually?" In the end, she made the important decision to keep living and fighting the disease. For her, continuing the search for treatment and other medical help was part of her ongoing effort to stay close to God.

In the face of death or when we look ahead to death, we find ourselves examining our lives and desiring to do the best we can all the way to the end. This means we must be prepared as much as possible beforehand for death and the decisions surrounding it. How would you approach making the following decisions?

- Do I want life support?
- Do I want to continue chemotherapy?
- Should I have this surgery?
- What do I want for my funeral service?

The intention of this chapter and the story above is to raise our awareness of the kinds of decisions we may possibly face with regard to death and dying. Also, it is meant to give some help in making these decisions or in assisting others who must make them. Some of these decisions will require a good deal of thought and planning; others will come at a moment's notice and will require a quick response. We will begin by considering a few suggestions about decision-making in general. Then we will focus on some specific decisions that need to be considered.

Making Better Decisions

Plans fail for lack of counsel,
    but with many advisors they succeed. (Proverbs 15:22)

The decisions we will be confronted with in this chapter are challenging to act on without help. The following suggestions are given in the hope of sharpening our decision-making skills.

Seek Counsel

The Old Testament book of Proverbs especially emphasizes the necessity and wisdom of getting good counsel

(Proverbs 15:22, Proverbs 12:15). If you have a terminal illness or condition, having a team of friends or family that helps you make important decisions is recommended. They can know your medical prognosis and your options, and can then offer advice about decisions you need to make or give feedback on areas you need to explore.

It is also important to have a medical team—friends or family you can trust with your prognosis and treatments and who can be available quickly, when you need them. Also talk to others who have experienced what you are going through. It helps to hear how they approached their decisions and what the results were for them. Pick advisors not for sentimental reasons but because they will be honest with you about your situation.

Have a spiritual team. They can help by bringing the Bible into the picture. Often you will need help with making decisions about certain things such as ethical choices, end-of-life directives, etc. Whether contemplating spiritual, insurance, medical, legal, financial or other issues, get help from those you can trust and have confidence in, who will help you make good decisions for your situation.

Obtain Sufficient Information

We need to make sure we have the whole picture before making important medical decisions, not just the opinions of one or two doctors. There may be numerous doctors involved in a patient's care, but they are not always communicating with each other. We have to be sure we understand the language being used with regard to our medical condition. The facts need to be clear to us, even if it takes painstaking time to define them. Many hospitals have ethics boards that people

can consult if they have questions regarding any ethical implications related to a particular type of treatment or to other
decisions that need to be made. It's our life they are talking
about—so we need to raise questions, question opinions and
understand things as best we can before deciding.

Keep a Humble Attitude

Be humble and stay humble. Decision-making is not easy.
People, crises and circumstances bring a high degree of ten-
sion and emotion to decision-making. We must be self-con-
trolled—not overreacting to new developments or opinions,
but determining to process information patiently. If we learn
to listen and tolerate different thinking, it may help us sort out
things in our own mind.

Spiritually, we need to pray that God will help us to keep
our mind clear and to rely on him to work things out for the
best. We can't let Satan try to "guilt us out" over decisions that
may not have been ideal. We must do the best we can, put our
decisions and requests before God and others, and then be
confident that God will work with the results.

Take Responsibility

In the end, decisions have to be made. If there are decisions
regarding our life, then we must take responsibility and make
them. In the end, we are the ones who must live with our
choices. We need to ask God to guide us and stay beside us.

Decisions You May Face

Advance Directives

"Advance directives" are directives that all of us, but especially the dying, need to consider and put in writing before

death. These predetermined directives can protect the dying from any medical procedures that would violate their wishes regarding end-of-life or emergency care and allow them to have what they consider an appropriate and dignified death. Although these issues can be difficult to talk about, many people can share their stories of unexpected tragedies and the ensuing decisions that were thrust upon them in the corridor of a hospital. Advance directives may spare you or someone else the anguish of making these difficult decisions in such a pressurized and emotionally-charged environment.

With the medical technology now available, doctors can often rescue a life from the most desperate circumstances. However, that life may survive only as a body and not as a functioning person. Advance directives are designed to allow an individual's choice and dignity to prevail in light of treatments made possible by this technology. They can be clearly spelled out in a document that communicates the dying person's decisions about medical procedures, treatments and more.

The following are an overview of advanced directives, summarized from an article by Joanne Lynn, M.D.:[1]

Proxy—this involves naming someone who has the authority to speak on the patient's behalf when she is unable to do so because her medical condition prevents it. It is called a "health-care proxy" or "durable power of attorney" and is legally binding. (This is discussed under "Power of Attorney and Healthcare Proxy" later.)

Resuscitation—"ambulance technicians and hospital personnel will immediately try to resuscitate anyone who collapses and is near death. However, resuscitation may not be desired if the collapsed person has been quite sick with an illness that is expected to worsen and lead to death. In order to keep anyone from trying resuscitation, the patient should ask his or her physician to write an order 'not to attempt to resuscitate' (often called 'DNR' for 'Do Not Resuscitate'). This order does not affect whether the patient can get hospital care or other treatments. Most states now provide a way to have an order against resuscitation put into effect when the patient is at home or anywhere else."[2]

Hospitalization—when patients reach a point in their disease when another test or treatment is no longer desired, they may decide that they do not want any further hospitalizations. They may seek input from their physician to avoid hospitalization except in order to alleviate suffering in some specific way.

Specific treatments—the use of treatments such as intravenous or tube feeding, intravenous fluids (hydration), cardiopulmonary resuscitation (CPR), mechanical ventilation (respirator), antibiotics, blood transfusions and kidney dialysis should be discussed ahead of time when possible. Patients' choices can be written down in ways that are enforceable by law. If patients are unclear about the merits of a treatment, they have the option of trying it for a specified amount of time until a final decision is made.

Financial issues—this is an area in which obtaining help and advice is strongly encouraged. The dying and their families may need to consider the cost of future medical procedures and whether or not the costs will leave the family in a difficult position financially once the death occurs. How the family deals with current financial situations and any options available to them may need to be thought through. Discussing it ahead of time can save a lot of financial heartache down the road.

Events near death—the family should understand what will happen physically and emotionally to the dying person at the very end. This type of information can be obtained through a hospice or books. The hospice worker can tell you what to expect in the end. This knowledge can help the family prepare and can also give them some peace about the final moments before death.

Five Wishes

"Five Wishes" is a document that states the care the dying person wants to receive at the end of her life. It is one type of legally recognized advance directive document. It is a document that, when completed as instructed, states

1. My wish as to the person I want to make health-care decisions for me in the event that I can't make them for myself.

2. My wish for the kind of medical treatment I want or don't want.

3. My wish for how comfortable I want to be.

4. My wish for how I want people to treat me.

5. My wish for what I want my loved ones to know.[3]

Completing this document can help the dying work through the end-of-life discussions they need to have with family and others. It sets up a plan that, when the time comes, will save the dying and their family from sudden, painful and difficult decisions and serves to honor people's desires regarding the way they want to die. The address for obtaining this document is listed in the resource section at the end of this book.

It is important to realize that this is a type of document that we should all consider having on file, even if we are currently in good health. If we were to have an accident or sudden illness, our families could be put in a position of making difficult decisions without knowing what our desires are.

Hospice

Hospice care is an alternative to hospitalization for end-of-life care. It is, in my experience, frequently misunderstood. Some see it as a strange, "earthy crunchy" home medical treatment. Others feel that it is the last straw in medical care, and that it's "all over" when a person is turned over to hospice. Neither view is true. To understand hospice we must understand a few facts. One, most of us will die in a hospital setting. Less than twenty-five percent will actually die at home. This is exactly opposite of what happened just a hundred years ago, when the vast majority of people died at home.

Today, hospital care in our country is designed to "cure" your particular ailment or to save your life when it is threatened by a serious injury or accident. Hospitals are not designed to accommodate or replicate the home setting or environment, nor are they intended for long-term care. Other facilities serve those functions. This is why many people have a difficult time finding closure and finishing life issues in hospital settings where "cure" is often pursued right to the end.

Enter hospice. Hospice is a group of medical professionals and volunteers who recognize that there is a time and place when *care* is what a patient needs, not *cure*. They facilitate the patient's and the family's need to be together at home, to finish any life issues, and to be surrounded by family and friends. Dying at home allows a person to feel more comfortable and gives more control over the quality of life. "The hospice philosophy recognizes that every person deserves to live out his or her life with respect and dignity, alert and free of pain, in an environment that promotes quality of life."[4] An example of this type of care can be seen in the recent best-seller *Tuesdays with Morrie*.[5] In it, a young journalist spends time with a former professor who is dying of amyotrophic lateral sclerosis (ALS), better known as Lou Gehrig's disease. It is a great example of how the time used for care instead of cure can produce some of the greatest and most meaningful moments in a person's life. The book's story is similar to Ira Byock's *Dying Well*, in which the dying find courage, peace and meaning in some of the most difficult circumstances surrounding death.[6]

More information can be obtained by contacting your local hospice or the national address found in the resource section at the end of this book.

Will

If you do not have a will, one of the first things you can do after reading this chapter is to pursue having one prepared. A will "is a duly executed document that takes effect at death. It is left by a person to govern the final disposition of real and personal property."[7] Many people procrastinate or simply are not convinced of their need for a will, but preparing one can spare survivors all types of trouble at death. It is not very expensive and does not take much time to prepare. If you do not have a will, the laws of your state will decide how to dispose of your estate when you die.

Every state has its own rules for how to settle a deceased person's estate and distribute her assets. This is primarily handled by a will. For instance, if your father died and did not have a will, and your mother is already dead, then his estate would be probated by the state. The state then retains a percentage of his assets for processing the estate (percentage depends on state law). In some cases, one-third of the estate can be kept by the state. Also, there can be issues of custody (children or guardianship), debt, property and more that must now go through the long and often difficult process of probate. It is difficult enough for people to experience the loss of a loved one. It only adds to that difficulty when they are subjected to court proceedings and a possible loss of income due to the fact that the deceased did not have a will. My advice to you is to be wise, be prepared and have a will drawn up.

Living Will

A living will is often created at the same time a will is.

> A living will is a legal document stating an individual's wishes regarding life-sustaining treatment if he or she goes into a vegetative state with no hope of recovery.... Unless a living will has been written and signed, medical decisions fall to the patient's doctors instead of his or her family.[8]

The purpose behind a living will is to allow you to make decisions regarding what kind of care you wish to have at the end of your life. If you do not have a living will or a power of attorney, medical decisions may be made for you by others. These decisions might not be what you would desire and could leave others with long-term emotional and financial burdens. However, be aware that neither living wills nor "Five Wishes" documents are recognized in all fifty states. You will need to find out what laws apply in your state.

Power of Attorney and Health Proxy

The durable power of attorney in health-care matters or "health proxy" is a person (or persons) who legally has the authority to make decisions for you regarding your health care especially if you are not capable of making a competent decision. It is said to be a stronger situation than a living will, which only contains a written list of directives regarding end-of-life care or treatment. The advantage is that with a durable power of attorney you have not just written directives, but also a person who knows your wishes and can legally represent your interests and make decisions if you are incapable of doing so due to medical conditions. This advantage is important when decisions regarding your medical care change from day to day. It is comforting to know that if you are incapacitated, someone is there to legally advocate for the decision you would choose.

Long-Term Insurance

Long-term insurance was created to cover the health-care expenses that Medicare and Medicaid do not. People are surprised to find out that many health-care services are not fully covered by Medicare or Medicaid or their personal insurance companies. The rise in life expectancy has resulted in longer periods of living with diseases and disorders that require skilled care. This in turn means greater expense over longer periods of time. When services are not completely covered, they become an expense for the family to bear. Obviously, there is a cost involved in buying insurance and certainly not everyone will be able to afford it, but you should know that it is an option available to you. To find out more, contact your insurance agent.

Guardianship

If you are a parent, single or married, you will need to work through the issues of guardianship. Make sure your decisions are documented legally, especially if you currently have an illness that could render you incapable of making a competent decision. An attorney can help you with the process. Also, make sure you seek good spiritual input. Deciding who will raise your children in case of your death is one of the most important decisions you can make. And again, all parents need to make this decision and have it legally documented, even if they are not currently in a life-threatening situation.

Post-Death Arrangements

A multitude of decisions need to be made after a death—the time we least want to make them! However, there are resources available to assist you during and prior to this time. Many sources, such as funeral homes, insurance companies or books can provide you with checklists of things that will have to be done after a death: choosing a funeral home, locating important papers, securing copies of the death certificate, contacting the life insurance company, Social Security and Veterans offices, gathering all current bills, filing state and federal taxes, for example.

Personal Decisions

The following is a list of other arrangements to consider prior to your death, if possible, so that others' grief will not be interrupted by having to deal with these decisions at the time of your death.

Cremation or burial. This is not a decision you want to leave for others to wrestle with; make your wishes known prior to death.

Funeral service. If you have any strong opinions about the type of service you do or do not want, let your family members know well in advance of your death.

Organ and tissue donations. One more thing to consider is whether you wish to be an organ donor. In the United States you may donate organs or your whole body for the benefit of others. After death in a hospital setting, your family will be approached about organ and tissue donation. This can be a difficult time to bring up the matter; however, it is now required by law in hospital deaths. For many, the decision to donate is a decision to give life to others. For you to have made this decision and communicated it to others before your death will be very helpful to distraught family members as well as those who stand to benefit from your decision.

Family Decisions

Some decisions will need to be made by the family after the death of a family member. If you are helping a family in grief, you can help see to these details.

Funeral service. Some of the decisions with regard to the funeral or memorial service are

- How would you like the service to be conducted?
- What is the best way to remember and honor your loved one?
- Who would you like to be involved in the service and how?
- Is music or other personal expressions (poetry, photos) to be a part of the service and how?
- How are people to be notified about the death?
- Are children to be involved in the service and how?

- Will there be a program to hand out?
- If there is a graveside service, will it be public or private?
- Will there be a reception after the service?

Obituary. This can include statements about the deceased's life, work and interests. It should include the name of the deceased, family members and other significant survivors. It can also note other things such as the request for memorial donations in lieu of flowers.

Other rituals. There may be other rituals that the deceased or the family may want included or performed after the death. This may involve something as simple as a time for the immediate family to honor the deceased or it could be as large as a public celebration or party in honor of the deceased.

God has always commended those who are prepared. These are all challenging matters to consider, and they are certainly very important. One of the many ways Satan schemes against us is to catch us unprepared. Spend some time writing down your preferences and communicating them to others close to you—or write them down for others to read. It is never too soon to prepare—start making these important decisions today.

Spiritual Notes

In 2 Kings 20, Hezekiah was told by God to put his house in order because he was going to die (although God graciously decided to add fifteen years to his life). We, like Hezekiah, need to consider getting our house in order. We don't need to be told that we are going to die soon. We should start implementing today our decisions about relationships, financial and medical contingencies, funeral arrangements and spiritual issues that will come into play when we die. Then, with these decisions made and documented, we can go about our lives for as much time as the Lord allows us to have—be it five days, fifteen years or longer.

Relationships

As Christians, we need to be righteous in all our relationships. Among other teachings, Jesus instructed us to "not let the sun go down while you are still angry," "settle matters quickly," "forgive daily," and "keep no record of wrongs" (Ephesians 4:26, Matthew 5:25–26). If we have old issues or conflicts that have yet to be resolved, we need to get help and advice, and address them now—while we still can. Left unresolved, they will complicate our death and make it difficult for our survivors to work through the emotions, regrets or resentment they are left with.

Life Goals

Many people have had dreams of going on a special trip or completing a certain project before contracting a disease. If this is your situation, do not give up hope. It may still be possible to complete that project or go on that trip you have never taken. Let others who can assist you know about your goals. Let this be a reminder to us if we are currently able-bodied to not put off doing things if we can plan to do them sooner. Take time to do the special things with family and friends. Don't allow the busyness of life to squeeze out what is most important.

Legacy

What will you leave behind? What will others remember you for? What will you leave spiritually to the church? Will it be a passion for excellence? A life of service? A heart for people? How about the Christians into whom you poured your life, who will continue to imitate your faith long after you are gone? This is the kind of thinking that needs to be part of our living now. What a great opportunity that God has blessed us with to be able to have salvation, to have an eternal perspective about life, and to leave a legacy for our family, friends and others to follow. We all need to consider what legacy we want to leave, and then allow that desire to give us direction and motivation in the day-to-dayness of life. However, if you are seemingly close to death, you will want to think very intensely about what you want to leave behind.

Leaving the closest and most significant relationships is the greatest challenge in dying. Whether leaving a spouse, friends or family members you need to consider what your departure will mean to them and how they will cope after you are gone. This can be extremely difficult if preparation time is limited, avoided or not possible (as in the case of sudden death). If you have the time and opportunity, you should make the effort to consider the impact your death will have on others. Doing so will allow your loved ones to cope with your loss much better after you are gone. Sometimes the best gifts a person leaves behind are the discussions, prayers and tears that occurred as together they grieved and came to terms with dying.

Other things you can do with your spouse or close relationships include having special times together such as a trip, retreat, looking through photographs or even a simple dinner alone. You may want to write a letter sharing your feelings or the most memorable moments you had together. You also need to consider how you will leave them spiritually. What do you want family and friends to remember you for spiritually? Will they remember your faith as well as your tears? If they see the effects of pain, will they also notice your contentment with God and joy as well? This is not to minimize pain or tears but to cause us to think about the legacy we will leave of how we faced life and death. The legacy left by a Christian should be filled with the spiritual virtues that God has made evident in our life such as faith, hope and love.

If you are a parent, one of the ways you will continue to live on after death will be in your children. Have you prepared your children not to just survive, but to be successful after your death? Spiritually, what do you need to consider by way of preparation? Do your children have relationships with younger and older Christians that you have fostered and that will be there for them after you are gone? If you are terminally ill, have you taken the time to see that your children are secure in their relationship with God and that they understand, to the best of their ability, that God is working with you in your situation? Pray with your children. This can strengthen them and also identify issues they need help working through. Think ahead. Are there other things you can do to prepare them for life, such as a video that they can keep, letters to be read at certain times in their lives, special times to pray with them, giving them a vision for who they can become?

Rights and Right?

Sometimes the greatest spiritual dilemma for us as Christians is discerning whether we have the "right" to make certain decisions. Do I have the right to make a decision about someone else's treatment because she is now unable to do so? Do I have the right to make decisions about my own treatment that might shorten my life? Do I have a right to communicate my wishes about my end-of-life care in advance?

If we are sitting around waiting for the "right" answer to these questions to float by, then we will be waiting for a very long time. The only right answer is that these questions can only be answered in the specific context in which they occur. Even then, the decision may not be easily and readily made. This is why we need spiritual advisors who can step into the moment with us and help us arrive at decisions with a spiritual mind-set. We will need to pray and study the Scriptures. We may need some time to investigate and ask more questions before making a decision.

Be aware that Christians are often confronted with many of these decisions by surrounding family members or the medical establishment. If you are in this situation, feel confident in taking the time to seek advice and counsel for yourself. Do not let others pressure you into making a decision that you have not had adequate time and spiritual help to think through. You do not want to live life regretting a decision that you let yourself be hastily "forced" into agreeing with.

Yet, even after doing everything "right" and making a good decision, you may still have doubts later on. You will not be the only one to feel this way. What can you do? The only thing you may be able to do is to trust God and turn it over to him.

We live in God's grace. You did your best, and when under duress and facing difficult circumstances, this is all that you can be expected to do. If you currently feel this way regarding a past situation, talk about it with others. They can remind you (especially if they were there) of what you were going through and the discussions that took place as you made your decision. This can remind you that you were acting as responsibly as you could and give you some peace of mind.

Cremation

The Bible gives no specific commandment about the disposal of the body after death. There are many instances of burial listed in the Bible that indicate this is an accepted means of disposition (Genesis 23:19, for example). However, the apostle Paul places the emphasis on our permanent body, the eternal one, declaring that the "jar of clay" that we now inhabit was designed beforehand to decay and decompose and only be a temporary structure for us (2 Corinthians 4:7; see also 2 Corinthians 5:1–4, 1 Corinthians 15:35–58). I tend to see things Paul's way and recognize that I have an eternal body that has already been prepared for me and that God will change "the temporary" into "the eternal" regardless of the condition of my temporary physical body. For me, the greater issue with regard to cremation is that it can eliminate in some situations the viewing of the body of the deceased, which can be instrumental in helping the bereaved to acknowledge the reality of the death. However, for many, this is the choice they make for various personal reasons. Also, for many cultures cremation is chosen in part because it is a less expensive way of disposing of the body.

Treatment Refusal

Before the 1900s we did not possess the medical expertise that would prevent death in many circumstances. Today we live in a world of antibiotics, trauma rooms, life flight helicopters and defibrillators. We can live longer and preserve life longer, but not without challenges, questions and concerns. We may be faced with the common question, "Can I refuse treatment that will not change the fact that I am dying but will only delay my death and possibly bring about other complications such as financial pressure on my family or a prolonged life in a debilitated state?" This is a tough question for a Christian—or anyone—to answer. Some go so far as to say that you are taking your life in your own hands at that point. What is right or wrong spiritually? Which way do you go?

To begin with, I would suggest that we must consider each situation separately. We would prefer to have a book, chapter and verse that specifically addresses this dilemma, but it is not that simple. There is no blanket Biblical approach for all available treatments. You must look at each one individually. For instance, the elderly, dying person facing this question may come up with a very different answer than the mother who has been told that her daughter is in a coma because of an accident, that there is no brain activity, that she has internal injuries that require surgery, and that the doctor's opinion is that she will not survive the surgery. Jesus did not deal in hypothetical situations and we would be wise to follow his lead. You must face your particular circumstance and do the best you can.

It is vitally important to think through end-of-life issues before they are immediately upon you. Jesus spent a long time preparing his disciples for his death. He prepared them to accept it and not be destroyed by it as best he could. Follow his example. Do not shy away from topics such as death, heaven and sickness. Let others know your decisions about end-of-life issues such as cremation versus burial, health proxy and your funeral service. Prepare others by communicating about your belief in God and your view of heaven. Help them now so that if you suddenly die, they will not grow bitter and resentful toward God and possibly lose their relationship with him or lose a chance at having one.

12
Hospitals, Wakes, Funerals and Memorials

Godly men buried Stephen and mourned deeply for him.

Acts 8:2

Most of us do not spend much time in hospitals. We feel awkward and ill at ease. *The hospital is a place for "other people," not a place for me or my family,* we think. We can be just as awkward and ill at ease at wakes, funerals and memorials. We are generally not in these situations long enough or often enough to get an overview of principles and appropriateness that we need to know. This chapter will give some tips on going to hospitals, and can help us know what is and is not appropriate—so we can be the greatest encouragement to those who are sick. These tips will be followed by some suggestions regarding wakes or visitations, funerals and memorials, all of which can provide a great comfort and support to the bereaved during the early days of grief.

The Hospital

Often people who have terminal illnesses spend time in a hospital. Part of helping them may include visiting them there. Many have never set foot in a hospital, much less an intensive care unit (ICU) or emergency room. If you have never been to a hospital, talk to someone who has before you go. Knowing what to expect (sights, sounds, smells and more) will prepare you to respond to the patient in an effective way and will set your own mind somewhat at ease. Likewise, if you know others who are going to the hospital who have never been there, make sure you help prepare them for the experience. The following are some suggestions on what to do when visiting the hospital.

- Respect the hospital's policies at all times, i.e. visitation times and cell phone usage.

- Respect the rights and situations of family and friends of other patients especially in waiting areas.

- Know what you can about the condition of the person you are visiting so you can have a greater degree of sensitivity.

- Depending on the situation, stop at the nurses station prior to entering a patient's room.

- When going into a room, knock gently and then enter.

- If the person is asleep, leave a note at the nurses station for him.

- When you enter, greet people in the room and know that it is okay to move next to the bed to speak to the patient.

- An appropriate touch (such as holding a hand) is important and can be comforting. Be careful about moving someone or getting the person to return the gesture if it is difficult. Do not sit on the bed unless you are invited.

- Keep the conversation appropriate, such as asking about his medical condition, lighter subjects (sports), what is happening in your life, etc. If he asks you to pray with him, ask if there is something specific he would like you to pray for. If not asked to pray, use your best judgment on bringing it up.

- When someone is in a coma, you can pray for or talk aloud to him. Many say that the last sense to go is a person's hearing. You can tell him you love him or pass on someone else's love. Reading to him can be comforting. Even if he is not alert or visually awake, he may actually be able to hear you or feel your touch.

- Never communicate to the patient any treatment plan, diagnosis, medication regimen or prognosis. Information of this nature will be shared by medical professionals, the family and those who are directly involved with the patient's care.

A few don'ts:

- Don't be loud.

- Don't become the center of attention.

- Don't joke in an insensitive way.

- Don't disagree with the doctor.

- Don't talk about *your* problems.

- Don't take personally the way the patient responds to you—remember, he is the one who is sick!

The Wake or Visitation

Understand the Purpose

The wake or visitation is simply a gathering of the survivors and a viewing of the body. For the mourner it serves a number of purposes, some of which are (1) coming to grips with the reality of the death (viewing the body), (2) the opportunity to express emotion, (3) the receiving of support from family, friends and community, and (4) the processing of one's relationship with the deceased through shared stories and memories. This is a time when the mourner is surrounded by family and others and reassured that he or she is not alone in dealing with the death, that life will go on, and that together, everyone can live through the loss. The purpose of the wake is to provide a time for the community to say good-bye to the deceased and to support those experiencing the loss most deeply.

Be Sensitive

The mood at the wake is generally determined by the circumstances surrounding the death and the cultural background of the family. If it was a sudden unexpected death or a difficult death, such as that of a child, it can be a tense, serious and emotional setting. If it was an expected death, such as the death of someone who had been seriously ill for some time, but had dealt with it well, the scene, though emotional, might be also warm, lighthearted and encouraging. Some wakes, depending on culture, may be more of a celebration or party atmosphere. Others might be characterized by loud wailing and crying. Whatever the mood, remember that people are in a state of grief. Let wisdom, not appearance, determine how you approach the bereaved and communicate with them. They may look upbeat, but inside they can be falling apart. Also, respect the *whole* family's mourning, even if the bereaved Christian seems to be more emotionally "up" and in control than others in his family. Different cultures have different ways of responding to loss and different approaches to funeral settings. If you are going to a funeral or wake and you are unfamiliar with the customs or rituals of the family, ask someone from that background what to expect and how to respond. You can also take your cues from the participants attending. Whether you are informed or not, remember that sincerity, respect and love will always be trusted guides in these settings.

Be Prepared

The wake is often the first time the family has seen the body of the deceased person since the death. This can be an extremely emotional time for family and friends. Be prepared for the intensity of emotions, and be careful not to overreact to statements and expressions of those grieving during this difficult time. Also, be prepared for any rituals that you may be unfamiliar with as discussed above.

Unnecessary Spiritual Comments

Never make comments such as, "How do you feel, knowing your brother [who died] wasn't a Christian?" Besides being tremendously hurtful and unloving, such comments can intensify the grief of the bereaved and harm your relationship with him and the relationship between his family and the church. Remember, you came to help, encourage and support the bereaved, not add to his grief.

If the question "Do you think my mother is in heaven?" is put to you by the bereaved, let him know that you feel it would not be appropriate to discuss it at the present time, but that you could meet with him some other time to talk about it. Encourage the person to use the wake and funeral time to honor the life of his loved one as best he can.

Follow the Rules

Wakes have simple rules to follow such as signing a registration book (for the family to know who was there) and passing through a receiving line and viewing the body. Please do not pass by others in the receiving line to speak only with the person you know. The receiving line is for encouraging and communicating to all the family about your sorrow and your connection to the deceased.

What to Say

As you are going through the receiving line or talking to people in the service, make comments that are appropriate for the level of your relationship with the bereaved. To those you know well, you may simply wish to express "I love you; I'm so sorry." To family members or others you do not know well, it may be helpful to say something like, "I knew your father from work..." and to share something positive about the deceased if appropriate and if time allows. Don't manufacture discussion. Be sincere. Think about what you would want said if it were you standing there. Humor is acceptable, but only at the suitable time and only if you truly possess that gift.

Not a Field Trip

Please do not use a wake to educate children about death and wakes. You are there to help the bereaved, not to help your son or daughter understand what wakes are like or how they are run. The best way to handle education is by properly preparing them before the wake and then following up with them after it to explain anything or answer any questions. Unless the wake involves family or close friendships, use discretion about children attending at all. If they were not in close relationship with the deceased, I do not recommend bringing them.

Dress Appropriately

Show respect to all in mourning. It should go without saying that T-shirts, shorts and casual clothing are not appropriate for a wake, funeral or a memorial service—unless this form of dress has been requested by the family for some reason (such as an outdoor service) or you are sure it is culturally acceptable.

The Funeral or Memorial Service

Understand the Purpose

The funeral is the more formal and public service involving the survivors, the community of the deceased and the general public. It can be described as a rite of passage when a definite change of life takes place. This will be the last time the bereaved are physically with the deceased. This time is a reminder that from now on they will not talk together, live together or love together. They will be separated and a passage will have occurred.

A memorial service is similar to a funeral, yet without the body of the deceased present. Usually the body is already buried or cremated. Memorials tend to be more of a celebration and commemoration of the life of the deceased. However, do not be fooled by the different type of service. Grief is there, even in the more upbeat settings. While I will refer to "the funeral" in what follows, most of what is written here applies to memorial services as well.

Emotionally, the funeral is a time of transition, when one life is acknowledged as having ended, and as a result, other lives change and continue on. Also, the funeral honors and commemorates the life of the deceased and serves to integrate the survivors back into the community of friends and family that will help each other live the new life that the death has created. The funeral is meant to bring comfort to the bereaved (1) by memorializing the life of the deceased, (2) by providing a spiritual perspective of the meaning of death in their lives, and (3) by bringing together support for family and friends.

Be There

The funeral is the hard day. Separating from a loved one is difficult and for many can be overwhelming. If you can attend the funeral, be there. Even seeing one familiar person strengthens the bereaved and helps them know that they are loved and are not alone in the midst of tremendous pain. It is good to attend the graveside portion of the service, if possible, because it can often give you a moment to speak to the bereaved.

Sometimes there are meals or fellowship times following the burial. These are times when you can talk, meet family, serve, reminisce and be with people. Many friendships have been created and much comfort given in the short but important moments spent supporting the bereaved at such functions.

Be Respectful

As a Christian, you will attend many funerals in which different religious rituals and traditions are celebrated. Sometimes when people die, the family will have the funeral according to *their* own tradition (perhaps the religion in which the deceased was raised), which may exclude your church's participation in remembering and honoring the deceased. This can be a hard since your church probably would have liked to celebrate the member's death its own way. You will have to accept these situations, and when possible, memorialize the deceased member in some other way—perhaps by having a separate memorial service with the church members.

Also, when attending funerals sponsored by churches or religious groups that differ from your own, you need to feel free not to participate in a ritual you do not feel comfortable with. Concerning such rituals, do not show your dissatisfaction or make negative comments to the family or the bereaved. Though you may have felt uncomfortable, this is not the appropriate time to speak about it. It may be that a particular tradition or ritual is the only bit of spiritual substance that the family can cling to on this difficult day. They need to feel your respect, love and support, not your criticism.

Children

If you bring children to the funeral, be sensitive to the family and cultural tradition. It is certainly acceptable for bereaved family members to have their children with them. However when it comes to your own children, they should not be a distraction. Crying and noise can be very irritating and disruptive during a service, particularly when emotions are raw. If bringing your children is the only way you can attend the funeral, then it is fine to try. But if they are disruptive, quickly remove them from the service and keep them outside rather than repeatedly coming in and going out. You can still be outside when the procession exits the building after the service and the bereaved may be able to see you then. Where cultural tradition supports bringing the children, then feel free to have them attend and participate in appropriate ways (see chapter 6 for additional thoughts).

Be Comforting

A hand on the shoulder or a hug at these times says more than words. Your presence and love is more powerful than you know. Years after a funeral, people still remember certain friends who came to support them, and they will usually feel a bond with them that is meaningful and special.

Serve

Funerals provide an opportunity for you to serve. You may be needed for baby-sitting, house cleaning, handling phone messages, mowing the yard, washing a car, helping with meals or a luncheon, making phone calls or even participating in the service. Serving can also take the form of sending flowers and cards, leaving a phone message, praying and following up in the days after the funeral.

You may be asked to help with planning the service or funeral arrangements in some situations. If it becomes necessary to do so, help yourself and the family by getting advice from those who have experience. Your support and encouragement may be needed by the bereaved to ask those directing the service (if appropriate and the family agrees) for particular things to be included in the service that would more adequately honor and memorialize the deceased. This is necessary when church rituals or traditions are more rigid and such requests are not the norm (for example, if a family member wishes to speak during the service). Ask, but do not demand or create a bigger problem for the family to have to deal with at this most difficult hour.

Take Care of Yourself

It is okay to show your own emotion and have your own feelings about the deceased at the wake and funeral. Make sure that you allow yourself to mourn and express your grief in a way that is best for you. Too often you can feel the need to "be strong" for others and not honor the feelings that you have for the deceased. Crying, laughing and talking can all communicate the depth of your love and respect for the deceased and can give family and friends encouragement and support at this most difficult time.

In summary, hospitals, wakes and funerals can be difficult to attend. However, they can be extremely important in providing support, aid and comfort to family and friends. Christians need to be aware of the possibility of encouragement as well as challenges in these settings. Going to the hospital can be extremely encouraging for the sick but also to their family and friends. Going to wakes and funerals supports the bereaved in making the transition to life without the deceased. In all of these situations Jesus has set a great example for us by having compassion for people as well as by serving them. May we imitate him and do the same:

> A man with leprosy came to him and begged him on his knees, "If you are willing, you can make me clean." Filled with compassion, Jesus reached out his hand and touched the man. "I am willing," he said. "Be clean!" Immediately the leprosy left him and he was cured. (Mark 1:40–42)

Epilogue

In the course of finishing this book my grandmother, whom I wrote about in chapter 2, died. She was ninety-five years old. I flew with my brother to Texas, rented a car at the airport and drove five hours before stopping for the night. The next morning we drove the remaining two hours to the little community where the funeral was to take place. Along the way we stopped in the town where our grandparents used to live and walked around the old farm where we had spent so many summers playing, building things, hanging out and occasionally helping out. The memories hung thick in the air, and we could have stayed for a longer time if not for the service.

As we arrived for the funeral, I tried to remember for my own sake what I've learned over the years about these situations. Then I stopped and told myself, "This is the last time you are going to see her; take the time to remember in any way you can."

The flowers were beautiful; MaMa was dressed in a pink dress (her favorite color), and a room full of old friends came to say good-bye. My cousin and I spoke about her and reflected on the many memories and the much love we had received from her over the years. We thanked all her friends for coming and told them how much it meant to us and would have meant to her for them to be there. So many of them had become our friends in special ways over the years.

After the burial we spent a few moments at the local community center talking and swapping stories. I used every minute to collect as many thoughts about her as I could from old friends. Realizing that this would be the closing of a life chapter for me, I didn't want to miss anything.

As we drove away I knew we were leaving for the last time. We would have no reason to come back here now, and even if we decided to at some point, there would be nothing left of the world that we had with our grandparents years ago. What we would have, though, would be the sounds, smells, thoughts, stories and so much more that will continue to live on forever in our hearts.

The last thought I want to leave with you is to encourage you to live life every minute of the day and appreciate the blessings that you have. Mourning is a journey that you can live through, even though the journey brings pain. The day I saw my grandmother for the last time brought me much pain, but I know that I will live on and keep her memory close to me always. God is with me in this journey, and I know that he will remain close to you as well.

I will close with a verse that I think should encourage every Christian facing the challenges of life and death and the mourning journey:

> "I have told you these things, so that in me you may have peace. In this world you will have trouble. But, take heart! I have overcome the world." (John 16:33)

Appendix
Multicultural Mourning

As the world population grows and moves around, we are exposed to a greater number of different cultures. The possibility of being exposed to various responses to death is therefore on the increase as well. The following are some thoughts and suggestions for you to consider if you encounter someone who has rituals and ways of mourning that are unfamiliar to you.

Don't Assume

First, don't assume. This is probably one of the more helpful pieces of general advice for dealing with other cultures. The naive thing to do when someone dies or you attend a funeral is to assume that you know what is going to happen based on your prior experience with death and funerals. However, the best approach to take when other cultures are involved is to assess the situation, rather than to assume. This means that you try and understand mourning and rituals from the viewpoint of their cultural background. For instance, you may attend a funeral where loud screaming and wailing are part of the family's public expression of grief. Although this can be disturbing or uncomfortable for you, instead of judging them, seek to understand why and for what purpose things are done. This can keep you from overreacting and allow you to participate in some manner that is appropriate for you—even as you seek to learn about the culture.

The same principle applies when you are working with someone from another culture who is dying or bereaved. Always attempt to understand what death means to them and how their grief is expressed by seeking answers to these types of questions:

- What are their rituals and traditions surrounding death?
- How does this culture view death?
- What is the family's role?
- What could interfere with grief and mourning?
- What are the culture's views concerning medical treatment and hospitalization?

This type of assessment will help you to overcome some of your own personal discomfort with cultural differences and can help you understand and meet the needs of others in a greater way.

Make Adjustments

One thing to always remember is that the funeral and rituals are for those surviving the deceased. The family has chosen rituals to help them begin the transition from the death to the funeral and back to living again. This may not be the way you would chose to honor the dead or celebrate a life, but you may need to adjust your expectations and feelings. Respect for other cultures goes a long way in helping those in need of comfort, healing and support. Obviously if there are traditions or rituals that bother you, do not violate your conscience or act in ways that go against your spiritual beliefs. However, being able to consider the culture and to accommodate differences gives you the opportunity to participate in the act of honoring the dead and shows respect to those who are bereaved.

Build Bridges

Jesus crossed many cultural boundaries. Instead of emphasizing people's distinctions or reinforcing their cultural positions, he brought them together and unified them. He taught us a lot about stepping into situations rather than reacting to them from his own Jewish standpoint. He built bridges that drew people closer to him. This effort ultimately paved the way for many people to follow God and be saved. God is intent on our learning the same lessons and being able to connect with other cultures. Especially during a time of mourning, when people often rally together, bridges can be built that can give comfort and aid and open the way for many to find God or deepen their relationship with him.

Ask

Cultural divisions can be social or spiritual as well ethnic. Regarding wakes, funerals and other arrangements, a Christian who is a close family member of the deceased may come to you for input regarding her participation in these events. For example, she may wish to speak, have something read, or participate in the service in a way that is not part of the traditional format. On the surface, these traditions, whether religious or social, often seem closed to any variance. However, a sensitive and respectful request that honors the deceased in a personal way may be welcomed by other family members and be allowed even in traditional religious settings. Simply encourage the person to make her request in a respectful way to those in charge of the event. Even if the request is rejected, there is nothing wrong with asking.

Support

In the years to come you may have many opportunities to support other Christians, friends or family from different cultures. When you are helping someone during the process of mourning, make sure that you ask questions, get information, and watch and learn as much as you can about the person's culture. This will enable you to be an informed helper who is sensitive to cultural nuances and differences and is able to serve and love without cultural differences becoming an obstacle.

About the Author

Certified in Thanatology (Death, Dying and Bereavement) by the Association for Death Education and Counseling, Dennis Young is a minister and grief counselor who conducts death, dying and bereavement seminars for churches and community groups. He serves as a volunteer bereavement facilitator in Baystate Medical Center's bereavement program in Springfield, Massachusetts. He has completed the Hospice Training Program on Death and Bereavement and training with the International Critical Incident Stress Foundation. He is also certified as a bereavement facilitator by the American Academy of Bereavement. Dennis's strong Biblical knowledge and compassionate understanding of people add spirituality and depth to his grief counseling. He lives in Western Massachusetts and is married with three children.

Notes

Chapter 1: Loss

1. Kenneth Doka, ed., *Living with Grief: Children, Adolescents, and Loss* (Washington, D.C.: Hospice Foundation of America, 2000), 22.

2. Joan Hagan Arnold and Penelope Busch Gemma, *A Child Dies: A Portrait of Family Grief* (Philadelphia: Charles Press Publishers, 1994), 5.

3.Robert Neimeyer, *Lessons of Loss: A Guide to Coping* (Keystone Heights, Fla.: PsychoEducational Resources Inc., 2000), 39. (quoting Edgar Jackson, no source given)

Chapter 2: Grief

1. Examples such as Joseph (Genesis 49:33–50:1), David (2 Samuel 18:33), Abraham (Genesis 23:1-2) and Jesus (John 11:35).

2. Charles A. Corr, Clyde M. Nabe and Donna M. Corr, *Death and Dying, Life and Living* (Florence, Kentucky: Wadsworth, 2000), 216. Quoted from G. May, "For They Shall Be Comforted," Shaloem News 16 (1992): 3.

3. Neimeyer, *Lessons of Loss,* 91.

4. Hope Edelman, *Letters from Motherless Daughters* (Surrey, England: Delta, 1996).

5. Therese A. Rando, *How to Go on Living When Someone You Love Dies* (New York: Bantam Books, 1991), 18–19.

6. William J. Worden, *Grief Counseling and Grief Therapy: A Handbook for the Mental Health Practitioner* (New York: Springer Publishing Co., 1991), 22. Corr, *Death and Dying,* 213–214.

Chapter 3: Mourning

1. Therese A. Rando, *Treatment of Complicated Mourning* (Champaign, Illinois: Research Press, 1993), 27.

2. Corr, *Death and Dying,* 220. Quoted from L. Siggins, "Mourning: A Critical Survey of the Literature," *International Journal of Psychoanalysis* 47 (1966), 14–25.

3. Elizabeth Kubler-Ross, *On Death and Dying* (New York: Scribner, 1997).

4. Core, *Death and Dying*, 221.

5. Worden, *Grief Counseling*, 10–19.

6. Rando, *Treatment of Complicated Mourning*, 43–45.

7. See appendix: "Multicultural Mourning."

8. S. Paul Schilling, *God and Human Anguish* (Nashville: Abingdon, 1977), 258.

Chapter 4: A Biblical Perspective

1. Lance Armstrong, *It's Not About the Bike: My Journey Back to Life* (New York: G.P. Putnam's Sons, 2000), 202.

2. Mark Sanders and Tia Sillers, "I Hope You Dance," performed on CD by Lee Ann Womack (Universal City, California, MCA Records, 2000).

Chapter 5: To the Bereaved

1. Earl A. Grollman, *Living When a Loved One Has Died* (Boston: Beacon Press, 1995).

2. Rando, *How to Go on Living*.

MY STORY (pages 109–113)

1. Jerry Bridges, *Trusting God* (Colorado Springs: Nav Press, 1988).

Chapter 6: Helping the Bereaved

1. Sandra Fox, *Good Grief: Helping Groups of Children When a Friend Dies* (Boston: New England Association for the Education of Young Children, 1988), 21.

2. William J. Worden, *Children and Grief: When a Parent Dies* (New York: The Guilford Press, 1996), 36.

3. The list in the following paragraphs is adapted from Therese A. Rando, *Grief, Dying and Death: Clinical Intervention for Caregivers* (Champaign, Ill.: Research Press, 1984), 151–153.

Chapter 7: To the Dying

1. Corr, *Death and Dying*, 152–154. Rando, *Grief, Dying and Death*, 209–222.

2. Armstrong, *It's Not About the Bike*, 101.

Chapter 8: Helping the Dying
   1. Corr, *Death and Dying*, 164.

Chapter 9: Helping the Caregiver
   1. Kenneth J. Doka and Joyce D. Davidson, eds., *Caregiving and Loss: Family Needs, Professional Responses* (Washington, D.C.: Hospice Foundation of America, 2001), 36–37.
   2. Corr, *Death and Dying*, 237–238.
   3. David Kessler, *The Rights of the Dying* (New York: Harper Perennial, 1997).

Chapter 10: Complicated Grief and Mourning
   1. Kenneth J. Doka, ed., *Disenfranchised Grief: Recognizing Hidden Sorrow* (Lanham, Md.: Lexington Books, 1989), 118.
   2. Norman Brier, *Clinical Commentary* (St. Louis: Elsevier Science Inc., 1999), 152.
   3. Ibid., 151.
   4. Dennis Klass, *The Spiritual Lives of Bereaved Parents*, (Ann Arbor: Edwards Brothers, 1999), 29.
   5. Rando, *Grief, Dying and Death*, 120.
   6. Kenneth J. Doka, (from his speech "Challenging the Paradigm," (Newton, Mass.: Mt. Ida College Summer Institute, National Center for Death Education, July 12, 2000).
   7. AIDS is an acronym for Acquired Immune Deficiency Syndrome. HIV stands for Human Immunodeficiency Virus.

Chapter 11: Decisions We All Need to Make
   1. David Reisman, ed., *On Our Own Terms: Moyers on Dying* (New York: Educational Broadcasting Corporation and Public Affairs Television, Inc., 2000), 14–15.
   2. Ibid., 14.
   3. Commission on Aging with Dignity, "Five Wishes" (Tallahassee: Commission on Aging with Dignity, 2000), 1.
   4. The Hospice Federation of Massachusetts, *Choosing Hospice, A Guide to Hospice in Massachusetts for Patients and Family Members and Friends* (Norwood, Mass.: The Hospice Federation of Massachusetts, 1997), 2.

5. Mitch Albon, *Tuesdays with Morrie: An Old Man, a Young Man, and Life's Greatest Lesson* (New York: Bantam Doubleday Dell Publishing Group, 1997).

6. Ira Byock, *Dying Well: Peace and Possibilities at the End of Life* (New York: Riverhead Books, 1997).

7. Life Insurance Management Association International, Inc., "What Do You Do Now?" (Hartford, Conn.: LIMRA International, Inc., 1999), 17.

8. Karen Hess, *The Family Handbook of Hospice Care* (Minneapolis: Fairview Press, 1999), 116.

List of Resources

Organizations and Support Groups

Aging with Dignity
P.O. Box 1661
Tallahassee, FL 32302-1661
(888) 594-7437
(850) 681-2010
www.agingwithdignity.org
fivewishes@agingwith
dignity.org

Providers of "Five Wishes"
document

**American Association of
Retired Persons (AARP)**
601 East Street NW
Washington, DC 20049
(800) 424-3410
www.aarp.org

Information on Medicare and
health insurance for older
people

**American Association
of Suicidology**
4201 Connecticut Avenue NW,
Suite 408
Washington, DC 20008
(202) 237-2280
www.suicidology.org
(800) SUICIDE (hot line: 24
hours a day)

Information about suicide and
local referrals to survivors
of suicide

American Cancer Society
National Office
1599 Clifton Road NE
Atlanta, GA 30329-4251
(800) 227-2345
www.cancer.org

Information and referrals

Bereavement Services
Gundersen Lutheran Medical
Foundation
1900 South Avenue
Mail Stop: ALEX
LaCrosse, WI 54601
(800) 362-9567, Ext. 54747
(608) 775-4747
www.bereavementprograms.com

A national leader in educating health-care professionals in meeting the needs of bereaved families when a patient dies in a healthcare setting, or when a baby dies during pregnancy or shortly after birth

The Candlelighters Foundation
P.O. Box 498
Kinsington, MD 20895
(800) 336-2223; (301) 962-3520
www.candlelighters.org
info@candlelighters.org

International network of support groups for parents of children who have or have had cancer

Center for Disease Control
National AIDS Hotline
(800) 342-AIDS (24 hours)
www.ashastd.org/nah

Information, referral services, and publications about HIV and AIDS

The Compassionate Friends
P.O. Box 3696
Oak Brook, IL 60522
(877) 969-0010; (630) 990-0010
www.compassionatefriends.org

International support group with local chapters serving bereaved parents and siblings

Department of Veterans Affairs
(VA) Office
(800) 827-1000, local and
nationwide
www.va.gov

Funeral Consumers Alliance
33 Patchen Road
South Burlington, VT 05403
(800) 458-5563; (802) 865-8300
www.funerals.org

Information on planning
affordable funerals

Growth House, Inc.
www.growthhouse.org

Information on life-threatening
illnesses and end-of-life issues

**Hospice Foundation
of America**
2001 S. Street NW, Suite 300
Washington, DC 20009
(800) 854-3402
www.hospicefoundation.org

Information on hospice

The Living Bank
P.O. Box 6725
Houston, TX 77265-6725
(800) 528-2971
www.livingbank,org
info@livingbank.org

Information on transplantation

Medicare Hotline
(800) MEDICARE (633-4227)

Information

**National Association for
People with AIDS**
1413 K Street, NW
Washington, DC 20005
(202) 898-0414
www.napwa.org

Information and referrals

National Hospice and Palliative Care Organization
1700 Diagonal Road, Suite 625
Alexandria, Virginia 22314
(800) 658-8898; (703) 837-1500
www.nhpco.org

For location of local hospice programs and related services

National Infertility Association (Resolve)
1310 Broadway
Somerville, MA 02144
(888) 623-0744 (help line—see times on Web site)
www.resolve.org
info@resolve.org

Information, education, advocacy and support for those experiencing infertility

National Organization for Victim Assistance (NOVA)
1730 Park Road NW
Washington, DC 20010
(800) TRY NOVA (879-6682)
(202) 232-6682
www.trynova.org

Information and assistance and support for crime victims

National SIDS Clearinghouse
2070 Chain Bridge Road,
Suite 450
Vienna, VA 22182
(703) 821-8955, ext. 249 or 474
www.sidscenter.org

National resource for information and referrals to local organizations and support groups for those affected by sudden infant death syndrome

Mothers Against Drunk Driving (MADD)
511 E. John Carpenter Frwy.
Suite 700
Irving, TX 75062
800-GET-MADD (438-6233); (214) 744-6233
www.madd.org

Information, education and support for victims, families and friends of a drunk driving incident

SHARE-Pregnancy and Infant Loss Support, Inc.
National Office
St. Joseph Health Center
300 First Capitol Drive
St. Charles, MO 63301-2893
(800) 821-6819; (636) 924-6164
www.nationalshareoffice.com
share@nationalshareoffice.com

National mutual-help group for parents who have experienced miscarriage, stillbirth, ectopic pregnancy or early infant death

U.S. Department of Health and Human Services
Social Security Administration
(800) 772-1213
www.ssa.gov

Bibliography

Albon, Mitch. *Tuesdays with Morrie: An Old Man, a Young Man, and Life's Greatest Lesson*. New York: Bantam Doubleday Dell Publishing Group, 1997.

Armstrong, Lance. *It's Not About the Bike: My Journey Back to Life*. New York: G.P. Putnam's Sons, 2000.

Arnold, Joan Hagan, and Penelope Busch Gemma. *A Child Dies: A Portrait of Family Grief*. Philadelphia: Charles Press Publishers, 1994.

Arnold, Johann Christoph. *Be Not Afraid: Overcoming the Fear of Death*. Sussex: The Plough Publishing House, 2002.

Bridges, Jerry. *Trusting God*. Colorado Springs: Nav Press, 1988.

Brier, Norman. *Clinical Commentary*. St. Louis: Elsevier Science Inc., 1999.

Brier, Norman. "Understanding and Managing the Emotional Reactions to a Miscarriage." *Obstetrics and Gynecology* 93, no.1 (January 1999): 151–155.

Byock, Ira. *Dying Well: Peace and Possibilities at the End of Life*. New York: Riverhead Books, 1997.

Chetnick, Neil. *FatherLoss: How Sons of All Ages Come to Terms with the Death of Their Dads*. New York: Hyperion, 2001.

Commission on Aging with Dignity. "Five Wishes." Tallahassee: Commission on Aging with Dignity, 2000.

Corr, Charles A., Clyde M. Nabe, and Donna M. Corr. *Death and Dying, Life and Living.* Florence, Ky.: Wadsworth, 2000.

DeSpelder, Lynne Ann, and Albert Lee Strickland. *The Last Dance: Encountering Death and Dying.* New York: McGraw Hill, 2002.

Dobson, James C. *When God Doesn't Make Sense.* Carol Stream, Illinois: Tyndale House Publishers, Inc., 1993.

Doka, Kenneth J., ed. *Living With Grief: Children, Adolescents, and Loss.* Washington, D.C.: Hospice Foundation of America, 2000.

Doka, Kenneth J., ed. *Disenfranchised Grief: Recognizing Hidden Sorrow.* Lanham, Md.: Lexington Books, 1989.

Doka, Kenneth J., and Joyce D. Davidson, eds. *Caregiving and Loss: Family Needs, Professional Responses.* Washington, D.C.: Hospice Foundation of America, 2001.

Edelman, Hope. *Letters from Motherless Daughters.* Surrey, England: Delta, 1996.

Gerstenberger, Erhard S. and Wolfgang Schrage. *Suffering.* Nashville: Abingdon, 1977.

Goldman, Linda. *Breaking the Silence: A Guide to Helping Children with Complicated Grief—Suicide, Homicide, AIDS, Violence and Abuse.* Ann Arbor, Mich.: Brunner-Routledge, 2001.

Fox, Sandra. *Good Grief: Helping Groups of Children When a Friend Dies.* Boston: New England Association for the Education of Young Children, 1988.

Grollman, Earl A. *Caring and Coping When Your Loved One Is Seriously Ill.* Boston: Beacon Press, 1995.

Grollman, Earl A. *Living When a Loved One Has Died.* Boston:
    Beacon Press, 1995.

Hess, Karen. *The Family Handbook of Hospice Care.* Minneapolis:
    Fairview Press, 1999.

Hospice Federation of Massachusetts. *Choosing Hospice, A Guide to
    Hospice in Massachusetts for Patients and Family Members and
    Friends.* Norwood, Mass.: The Hospice Federation of
    Massachusetts, 1997.

Jenkins, Bill. *What to Do When the Police Leave.* Northfield, Ill.:
    WBJ Press, 2001.

Kessler, David. *The Rights of the Dying.* New York: Harper
    Perennial, 1997.

Klass, Dennis. *The Spiritual Lives of Bereaved Parents.* Philadelphia,
    Pa.: Brunner/Mazel, 1999.

Lewis, C.S. *A Grief Observed.* New York: Bantam Books, 1976.

Life Insurance Management Association International, Inc. "What
    Do You Do Now?" Hartford, Conn.: LIMRA International, Inc.,
    1999.

Neimeyer, Robert A. *Lessons of Loss: A Guide to Coping.* Keystone
    Heights, Fla.: PsychoEducational Resources Inc., 2000.

McGuiggan, Jim. *The Power to See It Through.* Lubbock, Tex.:
    International Biblical Resources, 1989.

Oxford English Dictionary, Volume 13. Oxford: Oxford University
    Press, 1989.

Rando, Therese A., ed. *Clinical Dimensions of Anticipatory
    Mourning: Theory and Practice in Working with the Dying, Their*

Loved Ones, and Their Caregivers. Champaign, Ill.: Research Press, 2000.

Rando, Therese A. *Grief, Dying and Death: Clinical Intervention for Caregivers.* Champaign, Ill.: Research Press, 1984.

Rando, Therese A. *How to Go On Living When Someone You Love Dies.* New York: Bantam Books, 1991.

Rando, Therese A. *Treatment of Complicated Mourning.* Champaign, Ill.: Research Press, 1993.

Reisman, David, ed. *On Our Own Terms: Moyers on Dying.* New York: Educational Broadcasting Corporation and Public Affairs Television, Inc., 2000.

Schilling, S. Paul. *God and Human Anguish.* Nashville: Abingdon, 1977.

Silverman, Phyllis Rolfe. *Never Too Young To Know: Death in Children's Lives.* Oxford: Oxford University Press, 2000.

Strom, Kay Marshall. *A Caregiver's Guide to Survival: How to Stay Healthy When Your Loved One Is Sick.* Downers Grove, Ill.: InterVarsity Press, 2000.

Swindoll, Charles R. *The Mystery of God's Will: What Does He Want for Me?* Dallas: Word Publishing, 1999.

Switzer, David K. *Pastoral Care Emergencies.* Minneapolis: Fortress Press, 2000.

Wogrin, Carol. *Matters of Life and Death: Finding the Words to Say Goodbye.* New York: Broadway Books, 2001.

Wolfelt, Alan D. *Healing a Child's Grieving Heart: 100 Practical Ideas for Families, Friends and Caregivers.* Ft. Collins: Companion Press, 2001.

Worden, J. William. *Children and Grief: When a Parent Dies.* New York: The Guilford Press, 1996.

Worden, J. William. *Grief Counseling and Grief Therapy: A Handbook for the Mental Health Practitioner.* New York: Springer Publishing Co., 1991.

Yancey, Phillip. *Where Is God When It Hurts?* Grand Rapids: Zondervan, 1990.

Who Are We?

Discipleship Publications International (DPI) began publishing in 1993. We are a nonprofit Christian publisher affiliated with the International Churches of Christ, committed to publishing and distributing materials that honor God, lift up Jesus Christ and show how his message practically applies to all areas of life. We have a deep conviction that no one changes life like Jesus and that the implementation of his teaching will revolutionize any life, any marriage, any family and any singles household.

Since our beginning, we have published more than 120 titles; plus, we have produced a number of important, spiritual audio products. More than 1.3 million volumes have been printed, and our works have been translated into more than a dozen languages—international is not just a part of our name! Our books are shipped regularly to every inhabited continent.

To see a more detailed description of our works, find us on the World Wide Web at www.dpibooks.org. You can order books by calling 1-888-DPI-BOOK twenty-four hours a day. From outside the US, call 978-670-8840 ext. 227 during Boston-area business hours.

We appreciate the hundreds of comments we have received from readers. We would love to hear from you. Here are other ways to get in touch:

Mail: DPI, 2 Sterling Road, Billerica, Mass. 01862-2595
E-Mail: dpibooks@icoc.org

Find Us on the
World Wide Web

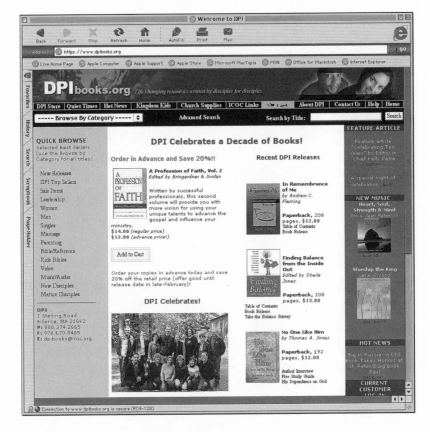

www.dpibooks.org
1-888-DPI-BOOK

Outside the US,
Call 978-670-8840